**F**

*by Ke*

MW00930374

Growing up in a time when a child was raised by the neighborhood, Kevin Jordan recounts memories of his past that now seem timeless. Personally reminiscent and still relatable, Jordan's stories make you, the reader, feel as if you grew up next door. Hilarious anecdotes, moments of sincere reflection, and a refreshing commentary on *how it used to be*, Jordan speaks to, and for a generation. Once you start reading this book, you will immediately start to reminisce about your own childhood.

Using snapshots of his memories, Jordan tries to make sense of an era when things only seem to make sense to those who tweet and #hashtag. Being raised in a time that was much simpler, Jordan still seemed to experience trouble as any typical young person when it came to school, his friends, and family, mostly because he was causing it. The stories he shares and the neighborhood that helped raise him reveal the impact an "old school" childhood has on his beliefs, philosophies, and outlook on today's technologically advanced world. The streets were his internet and the streetlights were his curfew. He takes you on a trip back to a time that you will remember yourself, or one that you would have enjoyed to live in.

Rather than pitting decades against each other, Jordan takes a fresh perspective in the generational debate to not just defend the way things were, but also respect the way things are today. His stories not only invoke nostalgia of times past, but also a juxtaposition that reaffirms the lessons of the past should not be lost. Even if you are too young to understand today, in a few years you will be reiterating everything Jordan has to say about growing up. Everyone else will just immediately know what he is talking about.

# Dedications

I would like to thank my mom and dad (aka Big Genie) for giving us the best childhood any kids could have. They instilled in all of us a sense of pride, values, and morals that we all took with us and passed on to our own children. They did without to make sure we always had. My mother would always say, "Shoot for the moon! If you miss, shoot again!" and "Put all your eggs in one basket. If that doesn't work, start another basket!" She always encouraged us by reminding us that it was never too late to "go for it." My father was the "neighborhood dad." Baseball, basketball, football, track, you name it, and my dad coached it. He'd take the whole neighborhood to games, and even pick them up and drop them off at their houses. Growing up the whole neighborhood knew my dad as "Big Genie." Now the whole neighborhood calls him "Grandpa." I guess now he's the neighborhood "Grandpa."

When I was young, I got into an accident in my mother's car, and she never got mad. When I was young, I broke my father's Lionel trains, and he never got mad (I don't think). When I got older, nobody was a bigger supporter of me when I quit the LAPD and started doing comedy than my parents. They are my biggest promoters and my number one fans. They gave me more than I can ever repay them in two lifetimes.

I love you. Thank you.

I'd like to thank my sister and brothers, Stephanie, Eugene, and Vance. We fought, we played, we fought, we laughed, we fought other kids, and we loved each other. There's an old saying: "Mess with one bean, and you're messing with the whole pot." That was the Jordan clan. We fought each other to the death, but nobody messed with us without messing with all of us. You made me tough, you made me smart, and you made me funny.

I love you. Thank you.

I'd like to thank Frank, Hopper (Hop), and Dave. We've been boys for over 45 years. I can't think of a time we spent together where we weren't having the time of our lives. We were thick as thieves and closer than family. We lost Frank way too soon; he was the funniest one of our group. I miss playing Strat-O-Matic!

Thank you. I love you guys.

I'd like to thank my kids, Kenny, Johnny, and Kevin. I tried to make everyday of your childhoods happier than everyday of mine. I hope I succeeded. You guys kept me young, and made me laugh. You still do! Pass it on to your kids.

Thank you, and I love you guys.

I'd like to thank my ex-wife Marilyn. We did a good job. I couldn't have done it without you. We weren't always on the same page, but we were always on the same team. Yes, you're my best friend.

Thank you. I love you too.

I'd also like to thank the whole gang on 113th road St. Albans Queens, New York:

Hopper, Frank, David, Lance, Barry, Rufus (Brother), Johnny Morgan, Margaret, John, Pop, Kenny, Mark, Wanda, Celeste, Veronica (Ronnie), Alisha, Lorrie, Keisha, Chubby, Jill, Tracy, Darryl, Woody, Karen, Abbey, Juliet, Karen, Janice, Denise, Bobby, Billy, Betty, Jeanetta, Tress, (Sandra), Bunt (Arvin) Gloria, Bert (Roberta) Stevie Creary, Judy, Donna, Lloyd, Suzanne, Richard Ross, Marla, Drew, Kent, Rodney Rose, Nadja, Zanya, Tony, Phyllis, Vincent, Richard, Robert, Irma, Paul, Gwynn, Mercedes, Big John. Zachary, Tony, Kenny, Anthony, Joey, Brenda, Will, Black Tyronc, Meo, Moosey, Earl, Evelyn, Moo, Horace, Dirty Junior, Carl, Winston (Winston Bent — he fought Mike Tyson...Goggle it!) Michael Bent (Heavy weight champ...Google it!) Melvin, Rosey, Dippa, Sunu, Benu, Brenda, Louie, Pancho, Michael, Curtis, Peaches, Vernon, Tim, Keith, James, Danny, Sly...

I know I'm missing somebody, but ya'll are not forgotten!

Thank you all 113th Road. Greatest block in Queens.

# Table of Contents

# Once Upon a Time...

I have a bad habit. Every five minutes I look at my phone. I have no idea why. I tell my son I'm addicted to my phone. Ever heard of FOMO. That's the fear of missing out. Well, I have FOMMI. The fear of missing my iPhone. I bet that's a real "phobia" these days and I know I'm not the only one either. There should be meetings for people like me. "CPA." Cell phone anonymous meetings, I think I'm on to something!

Ever be somewhere and someone's phone rings? Everybody checks their phone! Ever been a group of people and one of them takes out their phone and looks at it? EVERYBODY pulls out their phone! How Pavlovian have we become? One day I put my phone away. I wasn't going to use it, check it, or play with it for a whole day. Just to be certain I wouldn't cheat, I let the battery rundown. You know what I discovered after 24 hours? Nothing happened. The sun rose and the world kept spinning. I didn't miss a thing! Who knew? It taught me a lesson. Stop living life through a three-by-seven inch square. I vowed that day to put my phone away except when necessary. No Angry Birds, no Candy Crush. Nothing! How's that going you ask? Well, let's say, I'm getting there! One day at a time.

When I'm out and about I see kids that never look up during an entire dinner at restaurants. There's a famous Youtube video where a young girl walks into a fountain in a mall because she's too busy looking at her phone to notice where's she's going. Funny, but sad!

I didn't grow up with all this high tech stuff. The most high-tech toy I had when I was a kid was an Etch-a-Sketch! And the only thing you could make on that thing was stairs!

Then there's Facebook. Social media at its zenith! Anti-social media is what I call it because that's what it makes you. Anti-social! I use Facebook, but I don't base my life around it. Here's what I don't understand about people who post things on Facebook: do you think anyone cares what you're having for lunch? Stop posting pictures of your food! Do you think your cat is cute because you put bunny ears on him? Stop posting pictures of your cats! Do you think your world's going to end because your boyfriend didn't change his Facebook status from "Single," to "In a relationship" in the past 24 hours? Get a life! And NO, I don't want to share anything to show people I like you! NO, I don't want to use one word to describe the way we met! NO, NO, NO!

I was shopping for a tent to go camping. The next day all the ads on Facebook were tent ads! Then I was looking for a car, again, not on Facebook, but other sites. What did I see for a week on my Facebook page? Nothing but car ads! One time I had a dream of flying to Italy, The next day Facebook was sending me ads about discount airline tickets! You think this is what George Orwell had in mind when he wrote 1984? Is Facebook watching? Do they know? Here's another thing, why do people put all their personal business on Facebook? You can find out anything about anybody on Facebook. The police and FBI were looking for two guys for about a month that escaped from a prison in upstate New York. Just check their Facebook page. You'll find them!

It amazes me the things people will post on social media sites. They'll post nasty remarks about their jobs and their bosses, and then wonder why they get fired. They'll post their opinion on something, and then fight you tooth and nail with the nastiest posts if you don't agree with them. Remember folks, it's just your OPINION! The Red Sox stink! Am I right? Who knows, it's just an OPINION! The Knicks stink! Well, that's a fact!

I was watching a news program that showed a Rolling Stones concert. The whole audience had their cell phones and tablets in front of their faces! No one was watching the Stones, (who were right there in front of them) live! Remember when you'd go somewhere and just enjoy the moment? The surroundings? The feeling of being there? Not worried about how good your selfie came out! Remember when people would describe an event or a location they visited in such a way that it leaves such an impression on you that you remember it forever? It's like the difference between reading a book, or seeing a movie. Everyone will tell you that a book is always better because you have to imagine some of the things they're describing. The author has to paint a picture that you get to interpret any way you like. You don't get that with a selfie stick.

When I look back on my days growing up, I have some great memories. We did things, went places, and invented things. Growing up, I rode my bike all over New York City, without a helmet I might add. I won trophies for sports by winning, not just for showing up. Growing up, my friends and I went to New York Mets games, Knicks games, Coney Island, and concerts at Madison Square Garden (Parliament Funkadelic with Bootsy was one of my favorites). Life was outside away from the TV, way before the smart phone, and there was no internet.

Side story — I was at the Atlantis Resort in the Bahamas. I was standing next to a family of four checking in. The mother asked the desk person what they had to do for kids at the resort. The desk clerk told them they had the biggest water park in the Caribbean, a swim with the dolphin's adventure, one of the world's greatest walk through aquariums, and even a kids' club where they can build their own R/C cars. Then he said, "And we have free internet in the library." This is what got the kids excited! One of the kids even said, "Mommy can we go there first?" Beautiful beaches, a giant water park, swim with a dolphin, and a kids' club, but FREE INTERNET is what gets them excited. It just boggles the mind!

I remember the only time I was glued to the TV was when I was watching Saturday morning cartoons. Heck, I remember a time when TV actually went off. They just ran out of programming! First they'd show the late show, then the late-late show, and then they'd play the Star Spangled Banner and out! TV off! I remember watching black and white TV shows that were so good they're still on today. I defy anyone to find a funnier show than "I Love Lucy."

We went to the movies where an usher would walk you to your seats. It was also a time where you had respect for your elders, for no other reason than they were your elders. I saw a little boy run into a woman in the store and nearly knock her down. She told the boy to be careful where he was running, but was there an apology? No! The boy's mother defended her son's actions! "Don't talk to my son like that! You don't know him! He ain't your child. He don't have to respect you!" What can I say?

I like technology. It's made life a little easier and some of it is really cool. Although, where are those flying cars they promised us when I was a kid? But I do miss some of the simpler things. Things I don't see kids do anymore. You can't run in the schoolyard anymore because that's too dangerous. You can't play cops and robbers or cowboy and Indians — it's just not politically correct. AND you can't use your fingers as a gun because that's threatening. Really? Is a kid's finger loaded? Once upon a time kids could run and jump, ride a bike, go to the park, walk to a friend's house, talk to a girl…in person. Once upon a time you could, "like" something without hitting a button. You could climb a tree, walk along the top of a fence, eat a sandwich without worrying about glutens, GMO's or steroids, drink a soda without worrying about it making you fat. Once upon a time you could choose up sides and play a baseball game with every argument settled without an adult around. You could play in the street, walk to the candy store, stay outside all day until your parent's called you in for dinnertime, and spend a night catching "lightning bugs" (fireflies) and putting them in a jar. Once upon a time you could get served a PB&J sandwich and it wasn't considered "racist." Oh, that's a thing!

Once upon a time, there was a life before Facebook.

# Me, Me, Me!

I'm the last of four children. I'm the baby — mama's favorite — the runt of the litter! I've heard them all. What people fail to understand is, I'm a grown man! With children! And I still hear, "Oh, you're Helen's baby boy!" Not fun! Being the last child in most families means a lot of things: you're always going to get things last, you're going to get picked on, beat up, and disrespected by your siblings, and you have no identity of your own. In my lifetime I've been known as, "Little Vance" (my older brother), "Little Gene" (my oldest Brother), "Stephanie's little brother" (the oldest, and my sister). I could have been known as, "Little" Stephanie! That would have been really bad.

Being the youngest, most will agree, is a double-edged sword. First, there's really nothing you can do that hasn't been done, good or bad. Break something around the house? Intentionally or unintentionally, it has already been done by your siblings. Trouble in school? Your siblings have already done it, and probably with the same teachers! Miss a curfew? What's the response as the youngest? Vance did it too! Yes, we as the youngest love ratting out the oldest. I'll get back to that later.

To flip that coin over, win a Track medal? "Oh, that's nice! Just like your brother did!" Spelling bee? "You know your sister won that three times!" When an older child does something bad it is usually met with, "What did you do?" When the youngest does it, you hear, "Now what?" One of the good things about being the last child is parents are usually burnt out by time the youngest one comes along, so things the first one got a whooping for, the youngest just gets yelled at. I'll take that any day! Besides, the first child is kind of like the experimental child for the rest to see what works and what doesn't. Oldest child writes on the wall? What happens? Spanking, whopping, belt, whip, and an ironing cord. My brother once got beat with the big spoon and fork that hung on the wall in the kitchen.

By time the youngest child comes along, those parents are just tired! Worn out! The youngest child could set fire to the car, and what would he get? "Are you sorry you did it!?" Fine, FINE! Just go outside and play! Of course as the youngest you learn how to fake remorse! "SEE WHAT YOU'VE DONE!?" You just give them the youngest child sad face, maybe whip in a few tears, and you're gold! "Fine! Just go! Get out!" Works like a charm!

Second, there's a reason we're the favorite and it is simple. It's what I call the "Dinner Theory." The first child is like the entrée. The "steak" of the meal. The restaurant is named after you. Joe's STEAK House, Red LOBSTER, Olive Garden (if you consider that Italian!) That's why you came. For the entrée. The first child is the most anticipated one! You spend the most time choosing the name, and you have the biggest shower. People come from miles around to see that first child. Ahh what a steak!

The last child is your dessert. What do you say after the dessert? The same thing you say after the last child: "That's enough! I can't take anymore! Just bring the bill!" So what about the middle children? They're just the side dishes. No big fanfare, no big party, and no stressing over the name. In fact, most people just start guessing at names for the middle children. I wanted to name one of my children "ESPN" (pronounced "Espin"). Cool huh? Let's just say, smarter heads prevailed. By the way, if it was a girl, her name was going to be "Lifetime!"

The middle children are just the potatoes and vegetables of the family, and all a la carte! My buddy has seven children. When they got married they swore they were going to have two! Lucy, Sarah, Charlotte (they call her Charlie because they wanted a boy, didn't get it, and thought they were done), to continue: Marie, Nancy, Jewel, and finally Joseph. Tah-Dah! That's side dishes and soup too! As the old joke goes, if the last two had been twins, I'd have named them, "Get-off" and "Stay-off!"

Wish you were the baby of the family? Sounds like all milk and honey does it? Here's the flip-side! Like I said, first you have no identity. "Little Gene," "Little Vance," "Stephanie's Little brother," and the comparisons never ended! You're not as smart as your sister. Your brother was faster. My parents forgot my name so many times I thought my name was, "Hey you!" Also, back in the day, every youngest child knew this phrase: "hand-me-downs." For those of you who have never heard of this, hand-me-downs are clothes that your brothers and sisters got new, wore until they outgrew them, or were worn out, and then they became yours! Every younger sibling back in the day wore them too. In fact, most kids back in the day never got clothes that fit them! Parents back then bought everything that, as your mother would say, "You'll grow into!" Wear a size four shoe? They'd buy a five and a half! Why? Because you'll grow into them! Wear size 12 pants? Or size two dress? Think that's what you're getting? Nope! You're getting clothes that one day MIGHT fit! And if you were the youngest, you didn't even get new clothes that didn't fit! You got hand-me-downs that didn't fit!

At my house we had a closet in the basement. In that closet was everything my siblings ever owned, wore, or didn't like. So there was no reason to ever buy me anything new. If I said, "Mom, I need a new pair of pants," she'd say, "Go look in that closet you'll find a pair that fits you!" If I said, "Dad I made the track team! I need some track shoes," I'd hear, "Your brother ran track, go look in that closet. There's some shoes back there that'll fit you!" It got so bad one day that I had to go to school wearing culottes and saddle shoes! You'd think I'd have gotten bullied or teased, but half the kids in school were dressed the same way, so who was going to say anything?

# How Did I Get Here?

I played baseball. I was a really good player too! Centerfield, left field, and shortstop — I even got a letter from the New York Mets to come try out! But my sister was a great softball player. She could pitch and once batted over .800 in a season. .800! That's unheard of! I also played football, but my brothers played football too. I was good, but my brothers were *really good.* If you watch any home movie of us playing football, I defy anyone to find me. You'll see my brother's though! I was a gymnast in high school, and my brother Gene was a gymnast in high school too! In fact, he was so good, when I was competing at the City Final's I ran into his old High School coach. He recognized my last name, and even called me, "Little Gene!" That threw off my whole routine!

I ran track. I was fast! But ALL my siblings were fast! And they all ran track! Vance was so good, at one point he held the school record for the long jump and even won the Bayside High School MVP trophy when he graduated. I have to see that damn trophy every time I go back to my parent's house. FYI, I graduated Bayside High School with eight Varsity letters. Eight! (Three track, two football, three gymnastics) he graduated with four. Did I get MVP? I'm still hoping the Mets have my number.

Everything I've ever done or tried in my life, one of my siblings has upstaged me. From the time I was a kid, until I was an adult, it has been the same thing. When I became a cop, my sister became a corrections officer and rose to the rank of Captain. My brother Gene? He became a decorated NYPD detective. When I became a comedian? My brother

Vance had already done his third commercial and is a SAG member. I'm still waiting for both!

I remember one day I came home to New York from California for a family visit. I had just joined the Los Angeles Police Department (LAPD) track team and was in probably the best shape of my life. Vance came by and told me he was going to get back in shape and start competing again in some Track and Field events around the city. Sounded good. But he wasn't going to be in shape like me! I was in "LAPD track team" shape! Chasing bad guys and winning medals! So, the next day we went over to St. John's University and started working out. He was going to get back in shape? Maybe he'll look as good as me! We did some stretches, loosened up a bit, and then he says, "Let's do some 100-yard wind sprints." I'm up for that! Now, I've never beaten my brother in a race. *EVER*! But today was the day. How could I lose? I'm in great shape, and he's got beer coming out of his pores. This will be easy!

We lined up for the first race. He's slow off the start, but he passes right by me. You ever drive on the freeway and have a really expensive car go by you? The car isn't trying hard and it rolls by you so smooth it's like you're standing still? That's what it was like when he went by me. Okay, that was the first run. I'm not even breathing hard, and I got plenty left in the tank. We lined up for run number two. Again, I come out the blocks like a bullet. If it had been a 20-yard run, I would have won, but again he goes right by me leaving me in his wake. Run three, four, five, and I can't catch him. He's breathing hard, eyes watering, throwing up on the grass. He looks like he's just minutes away from collapsing. I wish! But he keeps getting up.

"Stay down Rocky!" How can he keep beating me? We aren't kids anymore. I'm a grown man! LAPD's finest! "Catch-em Kev" they called me on the department! But I can't catch my brother. I never beat him. Never will.

I helped him back to the car. I had to drive because he was too beat. A couple of days later I went back to LA. I so was pissed about my trip to NYC I quit the LAPD track team. I'll never forget that same night when I was on patrol, we got a call about some unruly kids. As we got there, one of them ran and I tracked him down in less than half a block. The kid says to me, "Damn you're fast! You're like my brother!" I looked at him, and said, "What did you say?" He tells me the only person who could ever run faster than him was his older brother. I un-cuffed him and let him go. I was afraid to ask him his brother's name. If he had said Rance, Lance, Chance, or anything else that sounded like Vance, I would have shot myself.

BTW…My brother is sixty years old. He still competes in Track and Field events all over the New York tri-state area and wins. He also coaches a girl's high school track team.

I took up golf. Unfortunately, so did he.

# So What Happened?

"I fear the day that technology will surpass our human interaction. The world will have a generation of idiots"
- Albert Einstein

I threw a birthday party for, well, for me! I do that a lot. "If you want to party, throw a party." That's what I say! Everyone was there: friends, family, my kids, friends' kids, everyone. All the adults are outside, and we're telling stories of times gone by, sharing lies we've now convinced each other actually happened. (Ask me to tell you my high school baseball story someday!)

During this party I noticed something very unusual. All the kids were inside either sitting in front of the TV playing video games, on the computer playing video games, on their phones playing video games, or talking. I shouldn't even say talking. I should say texting their friends on their phones. It looked like a pre-pubescent zombie land! No one was actually talking to each other, nobody laughing; I assumed they were all breathing because nobody was passed out on the floor. So what happened? Where did the fun of being a kid go? Had I become the old man my son always says I am? Had I become my dad?

My father told me he remembers one Christmas he was coming home from work and there were no kids out playing in the street. No one was bouncing a ball, no one riding a new bike, and on my block there were ALWAYS kids playing in the street, but more on that later. When my father came in the house we were all playing a toy he, uh, I mean Santa, gave us for Christmas called Pong. Pong was the very first video game to come out. It started it all. It was very simple. It was two video lines on the TV screen, and each player controlled one of the lines. A video "Blip" would go back and forth across the screen and you had a controller that controlled the line to block the "Blip from getting past you on the screen. It was like tennis, in fact, that's what that game was called. There was a switch on the console that added lines to the screen. One line was Tennis, three lines was Hockey, *and* there was a third switch that made the lines smaller, which made it Ping Pong! All three were the same basic game: a video "Blip" going back and fourth across the screen that you blocked with a line, but we had never seen anything like this! It was the start of the video game craze, but here was the difference between then and now. We didn't grow up with video games. We grew up outside running, playing, riding bikes, and climbing trees. We didn't need to be told to go outside. We WERE OUTSIDE!

From sunup to sundown, everyday of the week we were outside. Sundays were something special at my house. My mother would give me $2.25, I'd have to go to the store and get the Sunday N.Y. Times Newspaper, the Daily News and the Long Island Press. That's a lot of newspapers on a Sunday. It was heavy! When I'd get home, my father would have a stack of 33's on the stereo (Google it!) playing of all his jazz albums. Wes Montgomery, The Ramsey Lewis Trio, Herbie Hancock, Lionel Hampton, all the greats! Half of the neighborhood would show up at my house for breakfast because on Sunday, my parents would cook, and I MEAN REALLY COOK! Waffles, bacon, eggs, grits, sausage, pancakes, crab cakes, you name it. It was like a local diner at my house. If I had a game, I'd put on my uniform eat breakfast, and take off. If I didn't, I got dressed, ate breakfast, got on my bike, and took off. Either way, I was out the house and down the street playing with my friends.

The last thing you wanted to do when I was a kid was go *inside*! Every kid from my generation knows that if you went inside your parents would find something for you to do. Clean something, sweep something, go get something, and it wasn't an option either. So when you went outside, you got as far away from the house as you could. That didn't really matter because our parents had a network of people who always knew where we were!

Today the NFL has a program called "PLAY60." It's a program to encourage kids to be active for an hour. That's right, they have to encourage kids to play outside for one hour (I'll give you time to stop laughing). Could you imagine when you were a kid having to be dragged outside to play for JUST an hour? Just one hour? That would have been torture! From the time we woke up to the time the streetlights came on in the evening we ran around the neighborhood. And no one ever got tired! In fact, unlike today, we'd actually go outside and make *new* friends. A friend of your friend was your friend. We didn't need our moms putting us together on "play-dates!" Your mom has to find kids to play with you? What message are telling your kids? "I know you're too lazy to find real kids to play with you, so mommy will do it for you." Wow.

When I was in school they used to give out a "The Presidential Physical Fitness Award." (In New York they also had the "Mayor's Fitness Award") You had to run, jump, climb a rope, and throw a softball. (The New York one was harder because you also had to do the peg board!

Google it.) If you completed the events, you got a badge you could sew on your jacket. Every kid in school would have one of those badges. Everyone. That was the peer pressure of the time. You didn't get a fitness award? What's wrong with you? Even the fat kids would get an award. We had fat kids back then too, but the difference was they could keep up! It didn't stop there.

They used to give us the "Iowa State Tests." These were tests we took every year to test our reading, writing, and math skills. For us, these tests meant business! If you were in the fifth grade and the scores came in saying you were reading at a tenth grade level? You were the king! This was how we judged each other. If Robert got a physical fitness badge, I was getting that badge. If Susan was reading at a tenth grade level? I was going to read at an eleventh grade level! It was that serious. Nobody was going to outdo me. Academics and fitness were our driving motivations, not who has the newest Jordan's, not who has the best phone. It was about something that mattered.

We had scrapes, bruises, black eyes, bloody noses, fat lips, strains, sprains, raspberries, swollen fingers, swollen wrists, twisted ankles, bruised knees, broken bones, and heck, I played a little league double header with a broken collarbone! I dove for a line drive in left field, made the catch, broke my left collarbone, stayed in the game, and played the entire second game too! There was no ESPN in those days, so you'll just have to believe me. We could go all day!

Today? I once coached a little league team. A kid got a base hit, ran to first, and called timeout. He came back to the bench and asked me to replace him. Why? Because he was tired. TIRED! He ran to first! Good thing he didn't hit a double because he would have past out. If the timeline for evolution is correct, and we shed things we don't need (they say we as humans at one time had tails), then generations from now, humans will be born with no legs because kids today don't use them! I'm sure we'll evolve with big giant thumbs though. That all kids use now!

Think I'm kidding? My ex-wife's nephew was throwing a birthday party for his daughter. He told me that the party was at the local park and there would be a lot of games for the kids to play. I thought it would be fun to play kickball at the party so I went and bought one of those big red rubber balls we used to use in school. When I got to the park, to my surprise all the kids were already playing games. VIDEO GAMES! Her nephew had hired a truck that has a wall of video games built into the side of the truck. It was a big giant mobile video game machine! "Your kids are too lazy to play in the park? We'll bring the video games to you!" I couldn't believe it! (Ingenious on someone's part actually!) All these kids were doing was playing video games, but outside. Why even go to the park then? I guess if you're going to be lazy, at least you should get a little fresh air. The adults ended up playing kickball. We lost 28-22.

Here's a little test. When I was a kid they used to sell knee patches. These were patches that your mom would iron on to your pants at the knee because you ran, jumped, and fell so much that the knees of the pants would wear out. You'd see every kid with holes in the knees of their pants, or those knee patches covering the holes. The next time you're out and about take a look at a kid's pants leg. See if you see any wear and tear at the knees. I'm guessing no.

How can you wear out your pants' knees if you spend the whole day on your butt? When you find out, let me know!

How many times have you said to your kids, "Go outside and play!" Only to hear, "It's boring out there! There's nothing to do outside." "The sun makes me hot!" When I was a kid, I loved my backyard! My brothers and I tried to dig a hole to China once in the backyard. We got close too! I think part of the problem is kids have no imagination, they don't have to *make up* games. All the games they play require no friends, so there's no interaction with a *live* person. Everything is online. When you play the video game "Call of Duty" online, you're playing with, "Ramhead561," or "Locustflower16." You have no idea who these people are! Or if they're even kids!

We used to go outside, meet up with our group of friends and decide what to play. Every game we played was a running game, too! Tag, Freeze Tag (just like tag, except you couldn't move after you got tagged), Red Rover, Ring-a-Levio, Red Light Green Light, Hide and Go Seek, and my two favorites, "RCK" and "Hot Peas and Butter. Let me explain.

RCK is an acronym for "Run, Catch, and Kiss." The game was simple. All the girls would run, and then all the boys would chase them. If you caught one, you could kiss her. Get it? R-C-K: Run, Catch, and Kiss! (In the south they call it, "Hide and Go Get It." That must be the advanced version.) Here's how it really worked. All the girls would run from the base. The cute girls would run, but they were so fast that we could never catch them. The ugly girls would run, and then act like they fell so they could get caught! You didn't want to kiss an ugly girl! You'd just jump over them and keep chasing a cute girl! As we got older, we got faster. The problem was so did the girls. They were "young ladies" now, and they weren't about to be caught, unless they wanted to. Just like real life!

Hot Peas and Butter was another running game. Here's how it worked. Everyone would sit on the stoop. The "stoop" is the stairs in front of your house. (Google it.) Then one kid would go in the backyard and hide a belt, whip, an extension cord, or whatever we were using that day. Then he would yell, "HOT PEAS AND BUTTER! COME AND GET YOUR SUPPER!" Then all the kids would run into the backyard looking for the belt. As a kid got closer the person who hid it would say, "you're getting hot," or "you're getting cold," according to how close you got to it. So if you got close to it, he'd say, "You're getting hot, hotter! You're burning up!" Then a kid would find it, and he would chase everyone back to the base whopping them as he chased them. That's right, we made up a game where we would whoop each other! Crazy? Probably, but it was fun!

I saw a news report that a woman got arrested for (sit down for this one), "letting her kids walk a mile to the park to play." I'll give you a minute for that to soak in as you shake your head in disbelief. And it gets better! Okay, here's her story. This woman believes in letting her kids be "Free Range" kids. Know what that is? Of course not! It's a belief that you should let your kids explore, climb trees, run fast, fall down, get scrapes and bruises, fail at things, and basically learn things for themselves. Or as we used to call that: EVERYDAY!

"Free Range Kids." (Google it!)

Do you remember a time when you weren't climbing a tree? Falling and scraping a knee? Riding a bike without a helmet? That was just the baptism of being a kid! How many of us learned to swim by being thrown in the deep end? No "floaties," no swim jackets, no noodles. Just get in and start kicking. It was sink or swim, and we all learned the same way. Swimming might have been the only recreation that had a strict rule: "Wait an hour after you eat to go swimming so you don't get a cramp!" Why our mothers thought that eating and swimming caused cramping I have no idea! I always thought if we ate while we were IN the pool would solve that problem. The first time my wife said to me, "I have cramps!" All I could think was, "When did you go swimming?" I wasn't very bright.

I don't want to beat up on kids today — wait, can I say "beat up?" That's not very PC! As I was saying, I don't want to "belittle" (better?) kids today. They are very smart. Want your computer fixed? Call a kid! Need to navigate the Internet? Call a kid! Need someone to explain how your phone works? You guessed it, call a kid! The craziest part is, it doesn't even matter how old the kid is! My buddy's daughter plays games all day on the computer. She's three! She can't even read yet, but she can play any computer game and work an iPhone. Actually she taught me how to take better pictures. That's the truth! They've grown up with the computer, so it's all they know. I'm sure there will be a day when a mother goes into labor because her baby inside texts her, "Hey, Someone's draining the pool, I'm ready to come out."

I get it, it's a computer savvy generation. They text faster than I can talk. They upload, download, bump, synch, transfer, and they have a language I still haven't deciphered! OMG, BTW, TMI, LOL, BFF, IDK, ROFL, BRK, CUL8R (CUL8R — I had to ask around to find out what that meant). My son would close out his e mails to me that way. It means, see-you-later (C-U-L8R. Get it?) I thought he joined a cult at school! The C-U-Laters! I had no idea what it meant. I would say, well, when you get a chance, talk to M-O-M, he'd say, "What the heck does that mean?

"Call your Mother!"

"Ohhhh, LMAO!"

Here we go again! JSE. Just Speak English!

I love telling this story…

My son is a brilliant child. That's not just a proud dad bragging because he really is very smart. Stanford graduate and did it in three years! Phi-Beta-Kappa key winner as a junior. Very smart! One day he's flying home for the weekend and he tells me when he gets home he needs to go get his phone fixed. I say, "Okay, when you get to the airport, call me and let me know you're in." He says, "How can I do that, if my phone won't work?"

"Call me on a pay phone."

"Pay Phone? What's that?" he asked.

"A pay phone? It's a phone! Put money in it and call me!"

"Where would I find that?"

"In the airport! They're everywhere!"

"I've never seen a pay phone in the airport! Anybody can use it?"

"Yes! Anybody can use it!"

"Are you kidding? That's disgusting! I'm not using a pay phone! Just be there when my plane lands!"

After laughing all the way to the airport, I realized he was right! A payphone is a disgusting thing! How did we ever survive the collection of germs that would breed on those things? When I was a kid, they used to have phone booths! They were closable urine soaked booths that you'd go into to make a phone call. All the calls you could make and black plague you could endure for ten cents!
I guess it's a good things that kids keep the ball of progress rolling, but I just feel sorry for them that they miss out on so many things. Simple things. Playing catch with dad in the backyard, making a go-cart out of a lawn mower engine, putting baseball cards in your bicycle tire spokes so it would sound like a motorcycle. Cool kids used a balloon and it would sound like a Harley!

I took my son to a Billy Joel concert. (Actually he took me!) Real music, great concert, but the young girls who sat next to me never saw the concert! They were either texting, talking on the phone, or taking selfies. I actually heard one of the girls say, "Who is this Billy John guy? Is he new or something?" Shoot me! I'm sure they went home that evening and had no idea what they just missed — they just know they were there because they have "selfies" to prove it. But that's what they know. They watch the whole world go by in a 5x3 inch screen. Sad too. We had MUSIC! With real musicians! No auto-tune, no studio remakes, no lip-synching, just real musicians making real music. (Don't start me on that road now, but I'll talk about it later.)

When my son was ten, he tried to start an Internet TV show. Look it up. It's called "The Three Minute Lowdown." (All the news from the past week in three minutes. It wasn't that bad!) This was going to generate money for him to buy some new sneakers, err, I mean shoes! (I still call them sneakers.)

I told him when I was his age I wanted a new pair of Puma Clyde's. Those were sneakers named after Walt "Clyde" Frazier, who played for the New York Knicks — the coolest man to ever play in the NBA. Those were "Air Jordan's" before Jordan! To get them I had to get a paper route and earn the money. That paper route taught me responsibility, money management, accounting, customer service, and salesmanship. My son was quick to tell me that his Internet show taught him editing, green screening, blocking, hits, tracking and "Likes." Half of which I don't understand, and the other half I can't do. But, I do know this. Three months after I was a paperboy, I saved enough money and I bought those Puma Clyde's! Now that I think about it, three months after my son started that Internet show, he had no hits and didn't make a dime. I ended up buying him those Jordan's he wanted because he didn't make any money. Hmmm, who's really smarter?

Side story:
Just for giggles, I wrote down all the jobs I had before I was 21.
In no particle order they were,

Stock boy - Alexanders Department Store
Waiter - Catering hall
Salesmen - Macy's
Paperboy - Long Island Press

Vacuuming cars - Local car wash
Delivering and carrying groceries (we called it hustling)
Postal deliverer
Envelope stuffer
Soda salesman (sold sodas to softball players at the park)
Loan Shark – True, and quite profitable too!
Cable Puller - NY Islanders Hockey Team
Baseball/softball Umpire
Baseball Coach- NYC Summer job program - I just got the guys on my block to play for me.
Fireworks salesman - See Chapter 18
Mowing lawns

16 jobs of the ones I could remember. Ask your kids who many they had!

# The Country Squire Station Wagon

My current neighbors have two children. They bought a nine passenger mini van…for two children. In the mini van, my neighbor put four televisions in it to keep his two children entertained as they drive along. Again, just two children.

My dad had the biggest and greatest car ever made in American history. Cadillac? Nope. Pontiac? Not even close. My dad had a 1967 Ford LTD Country Squire Station! The greatest family car ever built! Olive green. It didn't have the fake wood paneling that every other station wagon of its day had. It had two full grown redwoods on each side. It was big!

There was a pecking order for sitting in the car. My mother and father were up front. The next row of seats was where my siblings sat. My sister always got a window, as did Gene, my oldest brother. Vance sat in the middle. Then way in the back, in the seat that faced in the opposite direction, this was my seat. Just about every station wagon back in those days had that seat. I bet that seat was 100 feet from the front seat. That's how big this car was! (Years later the neighbors got a station wagon where the rear seats opened from the middle and you faced across from each other. They only had two kids too! I guess when you have two kids you *think* you have "children issues." That doesn't really start until child three comes along!

We took every family trip in that car, and I hated that seat! Everyone else got to see where we were going, except me! The only time I knew where we going is when we backed out the driveway. The other reason I hated that seat was my father kept all his tools back there. It was like a rolling grease pit. Who wanted to sit in all that? But let's face it, given the choice between sitting in the front with your parents, or sitting in the back where the fun was, albeit the dirtiest place on earth, which would you choose?

We never wore seat belts back then either. I'm not even sure if those cars had them. Kids today buckle up like a astronaut heading to the space station! And yet we were just as safe back then as kids are today because my mom had a right hook that rivaled Muhammad Ali! If she was driving and she had to brake hard, or stop short, she'd throw her right arm out across your chest to keep you from flying through the windshield. And as if by magic, if my brother and I were up front with her? Her arm would extend out and stop both of us! How was that even possible?

I remember one day driving on the expressway, and the same exact Country Squire Station Wagon was driving right next to us. It was the same color, had the same wood on the side, and even the same amount of kids in the car. The only difference was they had a dog in the back of their car. A dog! I came to the conclusion that's what I was in the family hierarchy. The family pet! I remember looking over at that dog in the other car and him looking back at me like, "You too huh?"

Like I mentioned in the beginning, my current neighbors have four televisions in their mini van. One for each kid and two extra in case the kids bring friends I suppose. Heaven forbid kids talk to each other these days. (Talking is a lost art!) We had no such luck. We had to bring games with us on long car rides. Puzzles, Connect-the-Dots, coloring books. My sister always brought a Barbie doll. The SAME Barbie doll. She was always combing and brushing that doll's hair. She had literally combed and brushed all the hair off the dolls head! I think that doll had six strands of hair left, but my sister didn't care! She meticulously combed and brushed that dolls hair over and over.

Car toys were different from house toys. House toys were big, moved, and were noisy. That's what I liked. I wasn't allowed to bring those toys. My father always said, "You're gonna lose them if you bring them, and I'm not buying them again!" That was a rule my father had. If he bought you something and you lost it, he refused to buy you it a second time. Ask me how many phones my kids have lost and how many I've replaced. I understand that rule *now*. But I didn't understand the "lose them" rule *then*. Lose them where? In the car? The car was big, but I think I could find my Tonka truck in the car! Actually, when my dad sold the car in 1982, he cleaned it out and found not only my Tonka dump truck, but four GI Joe action figures, and a Stretch Armstrong. So I guess he was right! Any time we went on a trip you were only allowed to bring car toys. Like I said, car toys are books and puzzles, or toys that you were almost happy to lose! I didn't have any of those toys, so I had to make up things to play with in the back of the wagon. The problem was, I was back there sitting in my father's tools! The only things back there were greasy wrenches and hammers. I used to try to grab my brother's ears with a pair of pliers. He didn't care for that too much.

I had to be creative with the games I'd play. For instance, I'd wave at passing cars with a smile, and when they smiled back, I'd flip them the bird — the one finger salute! I'd like to add, my brother taught me that game. It wasn't until AFTER I got a whooping for it, did he explain what the "one finger salute" meant. Thanks Vance!

One day I found a roll of my father's good tape. For some reason my father had *good* stuff and *bad* stuff. I always remember my father asking us things like, "You see my good wrench?" Did he have a bad wrench? Or, "This isn't my good tie! Where's my good tie?" It wasn't until I became a dad that I realized that EVERYTHING I owned was my *good* stuff. I just didn't want my kids tearing it up! Once they get their hands on something, that's how it becomes the *bad* stuff.

Now, *good* tape was duct tape. Every man knows you can fix or make ANYTHING with duct tape. Many times I went to school with duct taped shoes, duct taped cuffs in my pants, and I even had a matching duct tape hat and belt!

July 14th, 1969. I was eleven years old. I will never forget this. I remember one road trip I had seen a James Bond movie earlier that week. James Bond gets duct taped to a chair, and the bad guys were trying to crack him for information. I figured this would be a great game to play in the car! I tore off a piece of duct tape and put it across my mouth like a prisoner. Then I put my face to the rear window and kept my hands behind my back. As cars would pass by, I would twist, turn, and pop up and down as if I was being held hostage. The looks on people's faces were priceless! I loved that game!

Once my brother saw me doing it. He thought it would be more convincing and realistic if he duct taped my feet together and my hands behind my back. It worked like a charm! Problem is, if you're hands and feet are taped together and your mouth is taped, you're pretty much trapped for real! It just so happened that day my father decided to stop at a place called Carvel Ice Cream. Everyone piled out the car, but I couldn't move! My father walked by the outside of the car and just stared at me in the back of the car rolling over trying to free myself. "Do you want anything?" I couldn't speak! I had a strip of duct tape across my mouth! "HMMMM! MUMMM!" That's all you can get out when you're bound and gagged! My father just turned away and went in to get ice cream! My mother too! She didn't even stop to look at me in the car! She just walked by and shook her head! You think my brothers and sisters helped me out? I think they secretly planned this! They ALL got ice cream. In fact my father even bought me an ice cream. A soft serve vanilla cup with rainbow sprinkles. The problem was, he didn't untie me until we got back home. So I got ice cream slop! That was the last time I played "car hostage."

Now, back to what I was saying. Every parent driving had two favorite sayings when they drove their kids around, "Do you want me to turn this car around?" And the other was, "Don't make me come back there!" Every kid I know from that era still has those two phrases ringing in their ears. If my parents were really mad we heard, "I will put you out right here!" That was the greatest bluff of all time!

The "turn this car around" threat never bothered me. Actually, from where I was sitting, I *wanted* my dad to turn the car around. I would finally get to see where we were going for a change! With the "Come back there" threat, I figured, "He's driving! What's he going to do? Pull over, stop the car and come back here?" Not my dad! Once that car was moving, we didn't stop until we reached whatever destination we were embarking upon. My brother once had to go to the bathroom. You think my dad pulled over to find a restroom? Heck no! My brother had to go while we drove down the parkway — out the window! Out the window at 65 miles per hour!

One day my brothers, sister, and I were being typical kids: loud, arguing, and fighting. What we call back then, "Monday!" Well, my father had enough. He gave us a double dose of *Phrase 2*: "You want me to come back there? Is that what you want? Because I will come back there!" Really? We had heard this so much we knew there was no meat on this bone! So in a voice just loud enough for my siblings to hear I said, "Well come on back here then!"

First, let me say, I was not a bright child. The fact that I made it this far in life is a miracle in itself. I do believe all the beatings I received as a child stunted my physical, mental, and emotional well being. (This is what I would say in court.)

Here's what I remember: just as I said it, the car went deathly silent. I could see my father's eyes in the rear-view mirror. They were red. Not a blood-shot red, but an "I've had enough, someone's going to die today" red. They looked like what you would imagine the devil's eyes would look like if you met him on a bad day and you stepped on his tail. He let go of the steering wheel and began climbing over the seat. He was actually coming back here! As he got over the seat, my mother slid into the driver's seat. I have never seen anything like this before, or ever again. It was like they rehearsed this maneuver over and over for just this day! We must have been doing eighty miles per hour down the road, and my mom transitioned from passenger to driver like socks sliding on a foot! Now she was driving down the road and my father was in my face in the back of the station wagon! "What did you say to me?" To this day, nobody in my family remembers this story. I know it happened. I think they were so shocked to see my father climb over a seat in a moving vehicle it just scarred them for life and they put that memory so far in the back of their minds it would take years of therapy to dig it out.

When I tell people that story they always ask me, "So what did your father do when he got back there?" Honestly, I don't remember. When he got back there I passed out. The sight of my father coming at me in a moving car was more than I could take. You ever wake up and have that feeling of euphoria and confusion? That's what I felt when I woke up. Everyone was back where they were before I passed out, and we were driving along like nothing happened. I was like Dorothy from the "Wizard of Oz." It was all just a dream. Every Thanksgiving we get together and sit around the dinner table and recall yarns of our youth. Every time I tell that story, someone in my family always says, "We don't remember that story, but we remember when you banged your head in the car and passed out!" I know what you're thinking, but I know that's a different story. I always look over at my dad when I tell that story and he always gives me a side look and a sly grin as if to say, "I told you I'd come back there!" And my mother gives me the look as if to say, "Yes he did, and he'll do it again!"

# Country Squire...There's more

My father always bought station wagons. We had a Chevy Belair Wagon, then the Ford Country Squire Wagon, and then a Ford Taurus Wagon. After we were grown, my father bought a Ford Thunderbird. When the engine blew on that car, he had a Station Wagon engine put in it. We took lots of family trips in those wagons. We would go to the beach in the summer. We'd drive all day then stay at a hotel. I liked hotel stays. Most kids do too! You could jump all over the beds, have pillow fights, and my parents wouldn't say a word. The hotel had a pool, which was cool too because we'd sneak out at night and swim around like we were doing something illegal. The next day we'd go to Rockaway Beach. My mother would pack a big basket of food and drinks. We'd stay all day at the beach, and then at night we'd walk up the boardwalk to the amusement park. Those were some great weekends! Years later when I started driving, I drove past the hotel we used to stay at when we would go to the beach. Then it dawned on me. All those years my parents would drive us all over town, as if the beach was far away. As it turns out, Rockaway Beach was twenty minutes from our house! Twenty minutes! They made it seem like we were driving across the country to get to the beach, but I could have taken the bus there in less than an hour!

When I got married my wife and I figured we'd try that with our kids. Plan a trip, tell them it's real far away, drive around town, stay at a hotel, and then go to the amusement park the next day. We drove around and then checked into the hotel. My son says, "I forgot my sandals." I wasn't going back home for any sandals, so I tell him, "We can't go back for your sandals, do you know how far we are from home?" He grabs my phone and looks it up on the GPS, "Two miles!"

I went home and got the sandals. Sometimes you just get outsmarted.

My mother loved going to the movies, but how do you go to the movies with four kids? THE DRIVE-IN! That's how! At least once a month my parents would load us all up in the wagon and head to Sunrise Drive-In out on Long Island. They charged you by how many people were in the car, so sometimes my brothers and I would have to hide down on the floor out of sight until my father paid to get us in. Once we got in the movie lot area we'd pull up next to a pole that had a big heavy speaker on it. Then you'd roll down your window and hang the speaker from the window. Someone told me years later that instead of the speakers, you'd turn to a certain radio station and the audio from the movie would come in on that station.

My mother would make all the food and drinks for all of us so we didn't have to buy anything when we got in. She would pop popcorn and put it in four individual bags — one for each of us. Vance would eat his real slow, and then when everybody was finished with theirs, he'd start bragging to the rest of us. "I got popcorn! Y'all ain't got none!" I always wanted to smack it out of his hands! My mother loved Cracker Jacks. She'd buy herself the big box of Cracker Jacks, and buy us the little box. Back then every box of Cracker Jacks had a prize in it. Sometimes you got a good prize, like a whistle, or puzzle, but sometimes you got crap, like a book. First off, the book was less than a half-inch big, so who could read that? Plus, what kid wants a book as a prize? Whoever got the worst prize my mother would give them her prize. Sometimes you got two books!

We'd always get there before it got dark. The movie wouldn't start before then. Right in front of the giant movie screen they had a little amusement park with rides. My father would give us all money to get on the rides. We'd spend half on rides and the other half on more candy and food! We had a car full of stuff, but that was homemade stuff. We wanted store bought movie candy! The best part about the drive-in was you got two movies! Where do you get that anymore? Between the movies they'd have a sing-a-long, a couple of cartoons, and a big giant animated clock telling how much time you had until the snack bar closed. I don't know why, but someone in the car always needed or wanted something during the countdown. In between every movie it was a race against the clock.

Sometimes we'd go to the movies on a weekday and we'd get to go in our pajamas. That way when we'd get home we'd already be dressed for bed. You'd see hundreds of kids running around the movie lot in pajamas. The other cool thing we got to do was sit on top of the car while we watched the movie. THAT was the coolest thing ever! Sitting on top of the Station Wagon under the stars watching a movie! Half way through the second movie I always saw cars all around us with fogged up windows and bouncing up and down. It was a long time before I caught on to what was going on! Hey, I was young!

One time going to the drive-in, my father forgot his wallet at home. The guy at the front gate told my father he had to turn around and head back out. My father turned the car around, but he noticed that the exit side to the drive in was wide open! So he hit the gas and we drove in the exit without paying. I was in my usual seat, in the back facing the wrong way. This night my father had made a big mistake. Most times my father would roll the back window down just a crack. "Just enough to let the gas fumes get in the car and put you kids to sleep," as he would tell us years later. (Who knew all that time he was just opening the window enough to poison his own children!) This night, my father had the window rolled all the way down, and as we attempted our stealthy maneuver to bypass paying for our evening's entertainment, we drove right pass a traffic cop. As we did, I yelled out the back window, "Hey mister, we're sneaking in the movie!" My father and mother both spun around fist closed and swung to knock my head off and shut me up. They didn't want to just shut me up, they wanted to shut me up for good! Unfortunately, just at that moment Vance stuck his head up to see what was going on, and he got the worst left-right combo punch from my parents that I have ever seen!

We got in the movie for free that night. Vance ate his popcorn real slow as he always did. Only this time, he did it because he had a swollen jaw.

# Under the Big Top

I hated the circus as a kid. When you're the youngest of four, the circus isn't a collection of incredible daredevils risking life and limb, or crazy clowns running around making people laugh. The circus is a big show of "what will we try to re-create at home" show. Every year my parents would take us to Madison Square Garden to see "Ringling Brother and Barnum and Bailey's 'Greatest Show on Earth Circus." First, we would see all the sideshows. My dad hated the sideshows because it meant he had to spend money. Chinese finger locks, tongue whistles, whips, and this was a *real* leather whip, too. We all got one! And we all got a pocket flashlight on a string, and when the lights in the arena went out, everybody would swing their lights around in a circle. What a fun day! But, then we went home.

Now my brothers and sister would want to recreate every act we saw at the circus. Let the misery begin. Here's how it would always play out. First my sister would say, "Let's play circus! I'm the ring master!" Then my older brother would say, "I'm the lion tamer, or I'm the trapeze man!" Get where I'm going? My sister would call the show, "Now ladies and gentleman and children of all ages! Let me introduce Geno, The Lion Tamer!" My brother Gene would come in the room and take a few bows. Now, of course if you have a lion tamer, you need? A lion! Who got to be the lion? ME! My brother would give me commands, "Lion! Get on the chair!" Then he would crack that whip on me. CRACK! Man that would hurt! "On the chair lion!" CRACK! I don't believe in violence or cruelty to animals, so I understand when animals turn on their trainers. "On the chair lion!" CRACK!

Here's what I wasn't allowed to do:
    1. Cry.
If I cried and my parents heard us they would take the whips away from us. (I should have cried louder!)
    2. Tell mom.
There was absolutely no snitching allowed, especially during home circus.
    3. Tell dad.
This was an absolute no-no. No matter what the situation, you could never tell dad what happened. Mom would yell and scream at us, but that we could tolerate. Dad enforced marshal law! If just one of us was acting up, we all got punished! If someone squealed on the others to dad? EVERYONE got punished! Even the snitch!

Lastly, you had to do what they said. Those were just the rules of the game. Actually those were the rules of any and every game. There was a few times I wouldn't play along, but you think Jewish guilt is something? Try sibling guilt!
    Stephanie - "Kevin doesn't want to play."
    Gene - "Really? I was going to give him some of my ice cream today!"
    Vance - "I helped you clean the room, and now you don't want to play?  Okay, I'll fix you! See what happens next time!"
    Stephanie - "I didn't even tell on you when that glass broke at dinner, but just wait 'til next time!" (I didn't even break the glass! In fact, I didn't do half the stuff I was blamed for, and I didn't even know about the other half of the stuff I was accused of doing!)

Gene - "Okay, if he doesn't want to play, don't let him play!"

I knew what they were doing, and I fell for it every single time, "Ok, I'll play."

"NO! You don't want to play, don't play. You ain't our real brother anyway, so go to your own family!" There's another story I heard my whole life. In the living room there was a family picture hanging on the wall taken BEFORE I was born. My siblings had me convinced for years that I wasn't a real member of the family and that I was adopted. It didn't help that when we'd go visit my parent's friends, my siblings would always tell me, "I think we're going to see your real family."

CRACK!

I HATED THAT WHIP! Up on that chair I would go, and my brother would say, "And now I will put my head in the lion's mouth!" Oh he would try too! Now it was Vance's turn. My sister would just call out random acts, and they would reconstruct the acts with me as the prop.

"And now ladies and gentleman, the Great Vancini doing the death defying acrobatics!" When I was a kid, I never knew what the phrase "death defying" meant. It actually means, defying death! Go figure. Apparently I had a death-defying childhood.

CRACK!

Now there was no reason for Vance to hit me with that whip, but if Gene did it, there was a 100% chance Vance was going to do it too! Vance wasn't as strong as Gene, but Vance had less patience. So if he said, "do it now," that's what he meant. He would have made a great Marine Drill Sergeant. Vance's trick this day was he was going to lay on his back, I was going to lean against his feet, and he would launch me high into the air, over the bed, and land softly onto a group of pillows on the floor. That was the theory. Here's what happened. The first time I didn't lean back fast enough and my brother just kicked me in the back, so I face-planted on the floor. After the second, third and fourth time, my brother pretty much realized that he really didn't have the strength to launch me across the room so here's what they did: Vance put both his feet on my left butt cheek and Gene put both his feet on my right butt cheek. Then they gave me a countdown. If you have older siblings the last thing you ever want to hear is a countdown. Nothing good happens at the end of a countdown. It is just their way of saying, "Prepare to die!"

5-4-3-2-1…Launch him! I would like to say I cleared that bed and landed softly on those pillows on the other side. I'd like too. I'd like to say I jumped up and took a big bow, but in reality, I don't remember what happened. I remember looking down at my sister as I flew by her, and I remember hitting my head on the ceiling light, but after that…nothing. I've asked them all what happened that night, but they all just shake their heads and laugh. No one ever tells me. No one talks about it. But I do know this. I'm not adopted. I think.

# The Three Musketeers

Growing up I had two best friends, William Hopper (better known as "Hopper or Hop") and Frank Venable. Hopper and I go back over 40 years and I talk to him almost every week. Unfortunately, Frank passed away. There isn't a day that goes by that I don't think about him. He was the funniest guy I ever knew. Funnier than me.

I always admired Hopper. He had it tougher than all of us. Hop was the oldest kid in his family. His mother always told him, "He had to be the man of the house." Hop had a father, but his father always worked, so every weekend Hop had to do all the family shopping, go to the laundromat, and watch his brother and sister's. Hopper was a lot smarter than all of us too. When we got older, he joined the Air Force and got transferred to Italy. Frank and I went to visit him and when we got there, Hop was speaking Italian! In less than a year he had taught himself Italian! He also had half the women in Italy and all the women on his base madly in love with him. He's a real charmer! I always tell him, when I grow up I'm going to be just like him!

Just like the true Three Musketeers, there were four of us. Dave Gallmon was our D'Artagnan. Dave came along later. He was a little younger than Frank, Hop, and I but he was still cool. Plus, he had a cute sister and his mom was like the neighborhood mom. We would go to Dave's house and stay there all day and night. His mom would make us lunch, dinner, go shopping for us, and even throw Super Bowl parties for us! (Thanks Mrs. Gallmon!)

When we were kids we were as thick as thieves. We did everything together. We used to love to play a baseball game called Strat-O-Matic. It was the original rotisserie baseball game. Hopper was a genius at that game too. You could tell him a guy's stats and he'd know what player it was. Any player.

"Hop, .327 batting average, 17 home-runs?"

"Joe Morgan!"

"Okay, 22-9, 243 strikeouts?"

"Tom Seaver!"

Side note, Frank swore he could hit Tom Seaver. Tom Seaver pitched for the New York Mets. Great pitcher, and to this day is the second leading vote getter in the Hall of Fame behind Ken Griffey Jr. (Until Derrick Jeter gets voted in!) Frank was a great batter too; he never struck out. NEVER! But he used to tell us all the time, "I can hit Tom Seaver." I still believe he could.

Whenever we would go to the park to play basketball we'd always hear, "Oh no, here come the Boston Celtics!" Nobody wanted to play us in three-on-three basketball. It's not that we were great shooters, or could jump real high (I could), but what we had mastered was *passing*. We knew if we just passed the ball and set picks, we would win! We knew if we beat someone off the dribble, the next time he got the ball he wasn't looking to just score, he was looking for revenge just to get even for being taken. So we'd double-team him, steal the ball, and score. How could no one else figure that out? Once we got on the court we'd be there all day!

The most memorable day we had was one Halloween — we were just out and about roaming around and then we ran into my brother's friends Joe and Anthony. They used to mess with us all the time because we were younger. (A few years after this episode, we're in my room playing Strat-O-Matic and Anthony comes in and starts messing with Hopper. Hopper finally got fed up and body slammed Anthony on the bed. He never had a problem with him again!)

This day, we were out "egging" houses. A very common thing to do on Halloween night. Joe asked me for an egg and Anthony asked Hop. Frank told us not to trust them, and sure enough they threw the eggs at us! I was furious, but what could I do? They were older than us. That's all I could think about all night. "How was I going to get even with Joe?" Later that evening we hooked up with the "Mangin Avenue Gang," and by gang I mean it was more like the "Little Rascal's, 'Our Gang,'" sort of gang. It was just all the kids who lived on Mangin Avenue out and about on Halloween night. Nobody had weapons, except eggs, and we weren't out causing trouble, except for egging houses. As we walked around, we saw the Keesville Avenue bunch; that's what they called themselves. They were all the kids that lived on Keesville Avenue. So there was "The Keesville Bunch" and "The Mangin Gang." We lived on 113th Road. We really didn't fit in with either, but we all knew each other so nobody really cared.

I bet there were at least 100 kids out there that day just walking the streets. The guys in the front of the pack would start running like they saw something, Hop, Frank and I would be in the back of the pack throwing eggs INTO THE PACK OF RUNNING GUYS! We didn't care! It was dark, and these weren't our guys anyway!

After wandering around for a while, we saw Joe and Anthony. Both of them lived on Mangin Ave. so they were considered "one of the guys." I could see Anthony playing around, and Joe was down on his knees acting like he was begging the guys for mercy and not to mess with him.

I was still furious. I said, "Yo Hop, there goes Anthony and Joe! You ain't gonna get them back for egging us earlier?"

"Naw, I'm just going to let it go."
I wasn't. I was still furious. I snuck up on the side of the street so Joe couldn't see me. Then like a Puma bouncing on it's prey, I ran at Joe who was still on his knees and smashed a egg right on his face! Now, as I've said in this book before, I'm not the brightest child ever to walk the earth. If you sneak attack someone with a "run-by-egging," the trick is to keep on running! Not me. I stopped, turned around, and yelled, "Yeah Joe, how you like that?"

From out of the crowd I heard someone say, "That's Kevin Jordan!" Then I hear another voice, and to this day I swear it sounded like Hopper's voice, say, "Yeah, let's get him!" Have you ever seen those movies where the town folk are chasing the monster through the town? That's exactly what it looked like! 100-200 kids were chasing me through the streets of Hollis, Queens! I remember I turned the corner and left the angry hoard in my wake. I was fast, but Joe was faster. Joe was gaining on me with every step. I never knew he was that fast. And mad! Every time I looked back at him I could see that egg actually cooking on his face! That's how hot he was! I ran to my cousin Debbie's house. I knew they always answered their back door so I slipped in that way. Joe never saw me go in. I looked out the front window and saw that mob of kids walking by. It looked like the young version of the million-man march!

I ran into Joe a few days later. I had told my brother Vance what happened, so he smoothed the whole thing over. It helps when everybody is scared of your brother. I apologized to Joe, and we were cool after that. That's the way it was back then. If you had a beef with someone, it got dealt with and then you moved on. No guns. No violence.

To this day, I play that day over in my mind. That voice yelling, "let's get him!" I'd still swear it was Hopper's voice! He always says it wasn't him, but he said when they started chasing me, he and Frank *were* running right along with them! He realized that they knew we were friends, so he didn't want them turning on him!

What's the moral of the story? Have lifetime friends for a lifetime. You'll always laugh.

# Mrs. Richardson & Mrs. Cramer: The Original Neighborhood Watch

On my block we all played in the street. That's what we all did. There was a park one block away, but you didn't always want to go to the park to play; sometimes you were told to stay in front of the house. Some games were just for block play:

Tag, Skully, Freeze Tag, Hot Peas and Butter, Hide and Go Seek, Ring-a-levio, Double Dutch (yes, I can still double-dutch), Stick ball, Punch ball, Ding Dong Ditch, Dodge ball, dirt bomb fight, Hopscotch, Box ball, Tooth ball (an 113th road original), Football, Whiffle ball, Red Light Green Light, Mother May I? (stupidest game of all time), relay races, roller-skating (you needed a key for these skates), and the list goes on. I'm sure I'm missing some, so if you have some, contact me!

One of my favorite games to play as a kid was Stoop ball. Stoop ball was simple. It could be played one-on-one or two-on-two. One team would be in the "field." One player would be on the curb in front of the house, and the other player would stand in the street.

The team "at bat" would throw a ball, either Pennsy Pinky or Spauldeen (Google it), and you threw it against the steps, or "stoop" in front of your house. If the team in the field caught it, you were out. If it landed in the street, it was a base hit. If it landed on the sidewalk or on the other side of the street, it was a double, and over the neighbor's fence across the street was a home run.

My house was the perfect stoop ball arena. There were no cars in the way and no trees to interfere, but there was one major problem. Directly across from my house lived Mrs. Richardson. She was Scrooge, The Grinch, The Wicked Witch of the West, and Gladys Kravitz, from the TV show "Bewitched," all rolled in to one! Mrs. Richardson would sit in her top bedroom window, which overlooked the street, and watch everything we did in the street all day, EVERYDAY! So if we were playing stoop ball and someone hit a home run, the ball would be in her yard. In fact, she was the only one on the block that had a fence around her yard. As soon as the ball would clear her fence, we all knew what would happen. First we'd look up at her window and see if she was there. I mean everyone has to go to the bathroom sometime, right? Then we'd try to be real quiet and open her gate, but we rarely made it. As soon as you'd lift the hook on the gate just a little you'd hear, "I SEE YOU! GET OUT OF MY YARD! LEAVE THAT BALL RIGHT WHERE IT IS! THAT'S MY BALL NOW! GET AWAY FROM MY GATE!"

Now actually, we could have opened her gate, gotten the ball, and ate a sandwich, all before she could get down the stairs and out to the yard to stop us. But we were very respectful kids. She was an adult — a CRAZY adult — but you showed respect for her. She would come to the front door and down the steps, still yelling at us, "GO ON AND GET AWAY FROM IN FRONT OF MY HOUSE! I TOLD YOU ABOUT PLAYING IN FRONT OF MY HOUSE! ...TRIXIE!" Trixie was her dog. She'd call the dog to get the ball, but the only problem was Trixie didn't have any teeth! As God is my witness, the dog had no teeth! So the dog couldn't hold the ball in his mouth! He'd pick it up, cover it in slobber, and it would fall back out of his mouth. "GET IT TRIXIE! GET THAT BALL!" She'd be yelling at us, and the dog would be trying to pick up the ball! "I SEE YOU JERDEN BOYZ! I'M GONNA TELL YOUR MOTHER WHEN I SEE HER TOO!"

She hated my brothers and me. She had this weird accent, and for some reason she couldn't say our name "Jordan," so she called us, "Jerdens." "Dem Jerden boyz." That's how we were known throughout Jamaica Queens. She would go everywhere and blame everything on my brothers and me.

My Aunt owned the neighborhood fish market, and every Friday it would be packed with people. Back then, Friday was fish day. Mrs. Richardson would go in there and tell everyone any lie she could make up and blame my brothers and me. "I saw dem Jerden boyz hanging round that store up the street. Next thing, the window broke. I know one of them broke it!" … "That street light on the corner went out. I bet it was one of dem Jerden boyz messin wit' it!" Remember the big blackout in NYC? Yup, she blamed us! "I saw dem Jerden boyz playing near that electric box on the corner; I know one of them pulled that wire. Probably that little one!" (Me!) Postal strike? "You know dem Jerden boyz are the reason they won't deliver the mail 'cause they no good! Especially that little one!" It didn't matter what happened, where it happened or how it happened, she'd tell anyone who'd listen, "Dem Jerden boyz did it!"

On our block, we were constantly under the watchful eye of Mrs. Richardson. She'd watch us like a hawk. Sometimes we would be away from our block, and we would still be up to no good! We always thought we were safe away from our block, away from Mrs. Richardson, but we weren't.

"I see you! I'm going tell your father when I get home!" This was the voice of Mrs. Cramer. Mrs. Cramer was like a roaming Mrs. Richardson. Same shrill voice, but without the accent. She actually lived two doors down from me, and I don't know how she'd do it, but she'd always catch us doing things away from our block. When she said "I'm gonna tell your father," she meant it! She'd march right over to our house and stick her head in the door. She wouldn't even knock! "Mr. Jorrrrdennnn!" She would singsong our name all the time. I remember one time she stuck her head in the door, and my brother was just walking by the door on the inside. Just as she stuck her head in and yelled, "Mr. Jorrrrrdennnn," my brother pulled the door shut. He almost chopped her head off. Almost.

The problem with Mrs. Cramer was she actually caught us doing things! Whether it was throwing rocks at busses, or putting firecrackers in the mailbox, she'd always catch us. She was a super snoop! The most famous catch she made was my brothers and his friend one night found some keys at a car dealership and started pushing each other around the lot. Not joy riding, not driving around the city, not crashing them — one guy would get behind the wheel and the other guys would push the car around the lot! That car lot was about three miles from our house, and it was late at night! How did she even see them? Well she did! And she turned everybody in! That was a whooping of a lifetime. I got whooped that night and I wasn't even there!

Many years later Mrs. Richardson passed away. My brother Vance started crying when he found out. After all she did to us, and all the balls she took away from us, he said she was still like family. I guess she was. She's was an 113th Road legend.

A couple of days after her funeral, her husband came to his front gate and started throwing out boxes and boxes of balls to kids. Spauldeens, tennis balls, hard balls. I even got my favorite football back that went in her yard 30 years prior. I felt bad for Mr. Richardson. He would yell at us too, but now I realize he was just a guy stuck with a crazy wife. He had to do things just to keep the peace.

Last year at my parent's house we threw a Barbeque. Mrs. Cramer showed up. At first we gave her a hard time for busting us all over Queens, but then we all thanked her for what she did. She was just looking out for us all.

It takes a village. You don't see that today. It's too bad.

# WTF?

I was at a friend's house for dinner. He and his wife are typical "Generation X Parents." Three kids, mini van, they have a house full of trophies for the kids, none of which are actually for winning anything, a Playstation hooked up to one TV, and an Xbox hooked up to the other, "selfie" pictures on every wall, and then something caught my eye. On the wall in the kitchen they had a chart. Here's what it had on it:

- Chores
- Obedience
- Homework
- Vegetables
- Honesty
- TIMEOUT!

Now, this chart had ten columns across, so lets say if you do your chores, you get a happy face in the column. When you get ten in one column, you get a toy. If you got ten stickers with a sad face in the timeout column, you got a five-minute timeout.

Let's start at the top:

CHORES! If the kids did their chores, i.e., clean room, take out the garbage, etc., they get a happy face. Hmmm, you get points for doing what you're supposed to do? We didn't get points; we got to live in the house another day. That was our reward! Every Saturday at my house, before we went out and AFTER Saturday morning cartoons (Hong Kong Phooey, Space Ghost, Fat Albert, Deputy Dog, HR Puff-N-Stuff...E-mail me your favorites!), we had chores to do. Wash, fold, and put away all the clothes, clean EVERY room, sweep the driveway, mow the grass, and rake leaves, which had to be the stupidest chore ever! Why rake leaves up when they're just going to fall off the trees again and again? AND then be covered by snow in a few months? All this had to be done before we went outside, and before our parents got home. Now, once you were done, you could go out, and the trick was NEVER to come around the house for the rest of the day. If you did, and one of your parents saw you, they'd find more things for you to do!

OBEDIENCE. This one puzzled me. My friends explained that if the kids did what they were told, when they were told, and don't have to be told three times, they get a happy face. (Are you sick yet?) First, this happy face thing was going to make me throw up. Second, let me get this straight, if you tell them to do something, and they ignore you twice, *then* you say it again, and now they do it, that gets a happy face? I can't stop shaking my head over this one! My parents would say something to me once — just once! My feet better had been moving! Sometimes they didn't even say anything; they just gave you a look! We all knew what the looks meant! Sometimes it meant immediately stop what you're doing, sometimes it meant do something right now! I'm 50 and my parents still give me the look! And my feet get moving!

HOMEWORK, HONESTY, TIMEOUT. You get a happy face for being honest? Really? Now you get rewarded for doing what you're supposed to do? "Hey ma, I put my clothes on and brushed my teeth! Give me a dollar!" I lied to my dad once. ONCE!

How come kids never have homework anymore? I remember we had homework everyday, AND on Friday we got *more* homework because the teacher said we had more time to do it! Remember when you had to write a report? Every family had either *The World Book Encyclopedia*, or *The Encyclopedia Britannica*. I once had to do a report on Christopher Columbus. What did I do? Get the "C" book and looked it up. Fredrick Douglas? The "D" Book. Let's face it, all we did was copy out of the encyclopedia. Thirty kids in a class all turning in the same exact reports! But to our credit, science has shown that reading something and then writing it down helps you learn it!

I saw my grandson "write" a report on Harriet Tubman in ten minutes! He Googled her on the Internet, copied and pasted her Wikipedia page, downloaded some pictures of her, and then printed it out. Done! I said to him, "Tell me something about Harriet Tubman" He asked, "Who?"
        "Didn't you just do a report about her?"
He says, and I quote, "I did a report about her. I didn't read it!" As they said in Ferris Bueller, "I weep for the future!"

Remember when you couldn't spell a word? Look it up in the dictionary! No spell checks in our day! You had to do the work too. If you didn't, your teacher would call home, and you got dealt with! And believe me, you wasn't getting a time-out! More like a "Knock-out!"

VEGETABLES. This one puzzled me at first. Then I realized that my buddy's wife can't cook! Why can't women cook anymore? I know a woman who tried to microwave a turkey! Here was the dinner menu she "prepared." Domino's pepperoni pizza, KFC chicken with mac and cheese, potato wedges, chocolate cake, Domino's Cinnastix, 7up, and Pepsi. Why both KFC and Domino's? One of the kids' doesn't like KFC. Why cake and Cinnastix? The other kid doesn't like chocolate cake. Just so you understand, this wasn't a special dinner at their house — this was a typical dinner! I love it when women tell me they don't have time to make dinner. Just for the record, my mother cooked breakfast, cooked dinner, worked, put four kids through college, went back to school, got her Master's degree in social work psychology, AND has been recognized by the U.S. Congress as one of the outstanding women in her field! You don't have time? Talk to my mother.

I digress. I asked, "Where are the vegetables?" His wife told me, "The kids don't like vegetables and won't eat them." Hence if they eat a vegetable they get a Happ…You know!

Where do I start?

I can cook. In fact everyone in my family can cook. You ask me to cook a meal, and I'll ask you, "What do you like?" I cook Thanksgiving and Christmas dinner every year. From the turkey, to the pie, and everything in between. (How am I single?) Do you know how I learned? I *had* to cook! When my parents were home, they made us get in the kitchen and help out. As we got older they would tell us, "Have dinner ready by time I get home!" And you better have it done too! Chicken, steak, fish, spaghetti, fried, baked, barbecued, rice, mac and cheese, and no boxed stuff! Green beans — the kind you had to "snap," — broccoli, cabbage. How many of you remember having to "clean greens?" I sat and watched my mom and dad (he's a great cook too) cook every meal when I was a kid. Best part? When they would bake a cake, they'd let you lick the beaters from the mixer. MAN! That was pure heaven! Sometimes my brothers and sister wouldn't be around and I got both the beaters and the bowl! SWEET!

I hated broccoli as a kid. But did I eat it? Never had a choice! You're mom would always start with, "Eat your vegetables. Don't you know there are kids starving in China?" Not the most PC statement, but I understand the sentiment. That would be followed by, "You're not getting up from that table until you eat your vegetables!" My brother Vance tried to hold out once with some green beans. He lasted two days without eating them, but then my mom made a green bean casserole for dinner. He didn't stand a chance.

I think dinnertime is a lost part of the family dynamic. Back in the day, everyone got called in for dinnertime. Sometimes we could go back outside and play, but only after the dishes were done. Nobody has dinnertime anymore. Kids make a plate of food and head back to sitting in front of the TV or computer. Then they dump the plates in the sink, or just leave them where they are, and get right back in front of the TV. We had to wash up, set the table, and then wait for everyone to be seated. After that, we talked, we would laugh, solved problems, shared stories, settled arguments and watched Vance stare at his green beans. But we did it together. That was the best part. I think Vance would be up to two happy faces by now on his vegetable chart.

# Get Out!

Have times changed that much? Do we really need to overprotect and micro-manage every aspect of our children's lives? Growing up there was no board in the kitchen mapping out my every task, activity, and event. When my kids were little, I used to make them walk to school. The school was only on the other side of the park, about a fifteen-minute walk. They would put up the biggest fit when I wouldn't drive them to school "Why can't you drive us! You know how far that is?" Granted it was an uphill walk all the way, but hey! It wasn't uphill both ways! There were dozens of kids making the same trek, so I wasn't worried that anything would happen to them. The kid next door to us put up such a stink about the walk, she got her mother to not only drive her to school, but she would knock on my door and take my kids too! I don't know where she is now, but I bet she's probably a great negotiator somewhere.

Think that's bad? When we moved, we lived right around the corner from my in-laws. You could see their house from our backyard. They were throwing a barbecue one afternoon and I told my son we were walking around the corner to his grandmother's house. AROUND THE CORNER! You would have thought I asked my son to walk across the Sahara Desert!

Maybe it's just what you grow up with. Hop, Frank, and I went all over New York City by walk, bus, train, or bicycle. Knicks game? We took the bus, to the train, to Madison Square Garden. Basketball game anywhere in Queens? Hopped on our bikes and off we went. I know it made us stronger, but I think it made us a lot more independent too! We weren't sitting around waiting on someone to take us, or do for us. We figured out a way to get it done ourselves! When I do shows and talk to people in there early 20's (Even late 20's and 30's) they're all still living at home! Where's that yearn for independence? That want for freedom? That, "I'm finally an adult" sense of being? I talked to one woman who told me she was adding a wing on to their house for their son. He drives a six series BMW and lives at home! I asked her, "Why are you building a wing on the house?" She said, "Because he won't move out!" How crazy is that? She's driving a Hyundai paying all the bills, and her son is living large in her house! Sad, sad, sad!

I have a friend who's fifty years old. He and his wife moved into a Del Webb retirement community. Now the rules of Del Webb stipulate that you can't move into their communities until you're fifty-five. Why and how did they move in five years early? He told me he was sick and tired of his kids moving back into the house, so they lied on all their paperwork so they could move in early. You see, at the Del Webb communities your children can "visit" you, but they cannot *live* with you. GENIUS! I think the best response I ever heard of for getting their kids out of the house was a couple told me when their last child turned eighteen, they sold the house and bought a Winnebago. They said they keep driving all around the U.S. and send their kids postcards from where they just left! That way their kids can never catch up with them. Brilliant!

My mother says that children today are late bloomers because they can be. There's no pressure on them to get a job, get married, and move out like back in the day.

Maybe. But, what happened to wanting to be self-reliant? Making your own decisions? Today, they get jobs, get married, and move back in!

In case you're wondering, I graduated college, had a job for six months, and then moved to California at the age of twenty-two.

I love when kids tell me how grown they are and still live at their momma's house. Move out! The scary part is, my oldest is about go back to school, the middle son is about to relocate to a new job and the youngest graduated college and is now "traveling."

I wonder which one is coming back first. I'm moving to Del Webb. Or I'm buying a Winnebago.

# Flip the Coin

We're all quick to jump on kids today for anything they do, or don't do! They're lazy, they feel entitled, no ambition, but I'll tell you what, I'm glad they're around when I need something done on my computer! This is what they grew up with; it's what they know. They are digital natives. They can't tell you anything about the Dewey Decimal System, but they can tell you how to upload your pictures and send them as a PDF. (I'll have to ask my son if that's right.) Their generation will never need to know how to read a map. It's all GPS now, so they'll never know what it's like to be lost. They'll never need to look up anything in a phone book — Siri will tell them! They'll never have to keep change in their pockets to use a pay phone. Spelling? Spell check! Of course, Y-O-U is now just "U," and "Oh my god" is now just "OMG." And, when we were kids, didn't we always hear, "Ain't" isn't a word? It is now!

They don't even learn cursive anymore. What for? The only time we use it is when we sign our names for something, and even that is going by the wayside. Times change, things change, sometimes for the better, and sometimes not. I remember learning how to fix a flat on my bicycle from my dad, but thinking "how dumb is he?" because I had to teach him how to program a VCR. I taught my son how to throw a curve ball, but he looks at me like an idiot every time I try to download a new app on my phone…or is it upload? The biggest problem I see with kids today is they have no social skills. They don't know how to interact with each other because they only talk to, or interact with each other electronically. I was watching the news on TV and the reporter claimed her child had a "Social Interactive" class. She explained this is a class that teaches children everyday social skills, such as how and when to say, "Please" and "Thank-you." The kids also learned the proper way to answer the phone, you know, THINGS YOUR PARENTS SHOULD BE TEACHING YOU FROM THE TIME YOU'RE BORN! The reporter didn't tell the story as if she was in disbelief that her child had to take this class — she spoke about it like she was proud! Wouldn't it be ironic if the class was taught online? I guess that would really be par for the course!

Today kids text, Twitter, Facebook, Tinder, Periscope, Instagram, Poke, Wink, Blog, Friendster, E-Mail, Hotmail, Instagram, and Gmail (my son made me get off AOL, and switch to Gmail). If you think things haven't gotten that bad? Look up an app called "Binder." Binder will send a snarky text and voicemail to your partner to break the news that you're officially done. It's like sending an insensitive breakup text on your own, but 100 times lazier. I think that says it all for this generation!

Remember the house phone? No one has a house phone anymore that the family has to share. I remember a kid calling my house to talk to my son. I picked up the phone:
"Hello?"

"Yeah, who dis?" the kid asked. "Who dis?" This was his opening line to me. Could it be anymore disrespectful? And this is the norm! My "old school dad" mode kicked in right away.

"I think what you meant to say was, 'Hello Mr. Jordan, this is Adam, may I speak to Kenny please?' Now I'm going to hang up, and you can call back and try it again."

I hung up the phone. A minute later he calls back.

"Hello Mr. Jordan, is Kenny home? May I speak to him…please?"

I think it stunned him, but I hope Adam remembers that day.

My friend owns a restaurant. He tells me kids have no idea how to come in and interview for a job. None! They show up late, don't turn their phones off during the interview, and then start telling him what it is they will and won't do at the job! When my kids would apply for jobs they used to tell me, "I can only apply online." I would tell them, "You go over there anyway, find the manager, or person in charge, introduce yourself, shake his hand, and let him know your intentions. Then you can go apply online."

By the way, all of my kids have careers and are out the house!

I miss the old days. We all do. It just seems like we had more fun and were more carefree then. I often tell stories with my friends that start with, "Hey, remember that time we all got on our bikes and went…" or, "Remember that time we were playing…" We just want our kids to have the same experiences. Twenty to thirty years from now how are their stories going to start? "Hey, remember that time we were on the Internet?" Really? A story about being online? I have friendships that go back over 40 years. Real friends! I know their families, their parents, even their dark secrets. I heard a kid bragging once that he had over 500 friends — FACEBOOK FRIENDS! Really think those are your friends? Ask them all for a dollar!

# We Were Dumb Too

It always cracks me up when I see the way things are labeled or done to "protect" us, well basically, from us! We have stupid labels on everything. "Do not use orally after using rectally." This was on an electric thermometer. "Do not eat." This is on the can of Play-Dough. (We all did that anyway!) And one of my personal favorites, "Do not consume if label is missing." This was written, ON THE LABEL!

I saw a television show that was talking about how harmful cartoons are for kids. "We're sending a dangerous message with all the violence." How dumb do they think kids are today? Do they really think they can order a rocket sled from a company called ACME and catch a roadrunner? Or a rabbit and a duck will argue over what season it was? "Rabbit season! Duck season! Fire!" Classic!

But. My father worked 20 years for the Department of Sanitation in New York City. He drove the Wayne Broom. That's the truck that sweeps the streets and curbs in every city. I rode in that thing many times with him! There's an old saying, "One man's trash is another man's treasure." Back in the day, my father would bring home "perks of the job," as he would call them. It was just things people in the city would throw away that my dad would bring home. He'd bring home some great stuff too! Sporting equipment, electronics, all sorts of stuff. One day my brothers found some golf umbrellas that my dad brought home. They were huge! They were two big blue and white umbrellas big enough that I bet if you jumped from a rooftop, you'd float to the ground! I could already see the wheels in my brother's head turning. "We need someone small and light." I could have run away. I should have run away! But I couldn't. I was equally as intrigued! It did make sense too! I'd seen it a million times on TV — even Mary Poppins floated in on an umbrella. It had to work!

Here was the plan. We would get on top of the garage, hold the umbrella, jump off the roof, and float ever so gently to the ground. How could that go bad? When I go back home to my parent's house now, that garage doesn't look that high, but back then it was like standing on the top of the Empire State Building. I was really scared. We climbed to the top of the garage and Gene opened the umbrella for me. "JUMP!" Vance had little patience, and even less compassion. I once saw him catch a bird in the attic and choke it to death with his bare hands.

"GO ALREADY!" It was a long way down; was this going to work? My brother Gene wasn't as crazy! "Ok, I'll give you a countdown, 10-9-8..." Just then Vance got behind me. "Just do it already!" He pushed me off the garage. In my panic, I let go of the umbrella and hit the ground hard — so hard in fact that I found out later that I broke my foot. Vance yelled down to me, "Why did you let go?" "Don't push me!" I snapped back! Gene was always the referee, "Okay, grab the umbrella and get back up here, and don't push him this time!" I limped back up on the garage. I was trying not to cry, as there's an unwritten rule that the little brother can't cry around the big brothers. It just ain't cool.

Attempt two. "Okay, this time when we count you down, you jump, got it?" This time I'd do it. Jump off the garage and float softly down to the ground on my throbbing foot. Here we go. 3-2-1. Jump! Needless to say, I didn't float to the ground. Heck, I didn't even land on my feet! I landed sideways on my hand and broke my wrist. "Are you alright?" That was Gene, the compassionate one. "He's alright, I know what went wrong, he needs both umbrellas!" That was Vance, the not-so-compassionate one. Now with my foot throbbing, and wrist aching, I had to admit, what he said did make sense. Two umbrellas would be better than one! As I said earlier, I wasn't the brightest of children.

So again I got on the roof, this time with two umbrellas determined to defy the laws of gravity, jump gracefully from the garage, and float ever so slowly to the ground below. The countdown began, 10-9-8... Just then my mother was pulling the car into the driveway. This was my chance! I was going to jump from the garage, land on the ground, impress my mother, and solidify myself as my mother's favorite due to my awesomeness!

...3-2-1... "Hey Ma, watch this!" As I jumped I could see my mother's face behind the wheel of the car. I've never seen a person's eyes get so big! As my feet left the roof of the garage, I saw my mother leap from the car and run towards the garage. My mother is five-feet one-inch tall, maybe 100 pounds, maybe. That day it was like watching Jackie Joyner-Kersey run towards me. She covered a distance of about 30 yards, in less than two seconds. It was like seeing Willie Mays dive for a short line drive into centerfield. She scooped me up just before my head hit the ground.

When we got to the emergency room, she was still yelling at me and my brothers, and they weren't even there! Five hours later that night when we got home, my mother was still yelling. My left hand and right foot were in casts. My father just looked at me and shook his head. He had tears coming down his face, and was biting his lip really hard. I know he wanted to say something. I'd like to believe to this day he was really sad and wanted to say something comforting, but I have a strong suspicion I'm wrong.

Six weeks after that day, my father brought home two beach umbrellas. They were huge.

I can still hear my mother yelling. And my father's lip never healed.

# Dads

In my neighborhood, sports were everything. We played any and every sport: basketball, tennis, and football, but baseball was king! We'd play baseball all day and all night long. Every spring, summer, and fall we'd play in the Catholic Church League for St. Pascal's even though none of us went to church, let alone St. Pascal's! We made our friend Lance become an alter boy so we could get our schedule and equipment for the week. Tuesdays and Thursdays we played in the CYO league (Catholic Youth Organization), and on Saturdays and Sundays we played in the PAL (Police Athletic League). Now you would think that would be a lot of pressure on our parents to get us to all the games. Nope. Our parents never came! We didn't care if our parents were there with after game snacks. We weren't playing for them. We played because we loved to play! Hell, for most of our games we didn't even have a coach! We'd get on our bikes and ride to wherever the games were. When the umpires would ask, "Where's your coach?" We'd say, "Oh, he's on his way!" We knew there was nobody coming!

Every game both teams were required to supply two new baseballs. We didn't always have new balls, so from time to time we would send one of the team's benchwarmers to "Time Square Department Store" on Farmers Boulevard to steal a ball if he wanted to play that week. Sometimes if the game was too far away, we'd take the bus and train. We'd be in our uniforms, lugging all that equipment: bases, balls, bats, and helmets, but that's' how dedicated we were to playing.

One day we were running late to a game and we hitchhiked. No kidding! Some guy with a station wagon came by, we flagged him down, and he drove us to our game! (Creedmore, for those of you in Queens.) Were we worried? Heck no. What was he going to do? We were ten kids with a bag full of wooden bats late for a game. I think HE should have been worried!

On the end of our block, there were some guys who started a taxi stand. They were just some adults that would take people mostly to the subway station, but they'd make a few bucks and drink all day. They were the original Uber! Sometimes they would see us heading out to the bus stop and for two dollars a piece they would drive us to the park, wait while we played the game, (drinking the whole time), and then drive us home! That's how much we loved playing!

A couple of years later Lance's father took over driving us to games and became our coach. He bought a fifteen-passenger van and new uniforms for us. (Philadelphia Phillies — baby blue road uniforms, with our names on the back! Damn, we looked good!) He even took over paying our umpire fees. Up until then we would all have to bring three dollars each. That really was an amazing thing Mr. Stanley did for us. But that was the way people were — they did things for each other back then.

During the year, my father used to pile all the neighborhood kids into the Country Squire Station Wagon for football, track, softball or anywhere they need to go. After every game, Dave's mom would feed us all, and let us sit around her house all day eating her out of house and home. The old saying, "It takes a village?" That was 113th

Road. All the baseball leagues stopped at 16 years old. So we would get fake birthday certificates and just keep playing! You'd think the other teams would catch on, but they were doing the same thing! No one cared. It was just about playing baseball!

My father played softball. He loved softball. His favorite was unlimited slow-pitch. That meant when you pitched the ball, you could throw the ball as high as you wanted. Most leagues are what they call three-to-ten. (The pitch has to be at least three feet high and no higher than 10 feet.) My father would throw the ball so high that he could back up behind second base before the ball came down to the batter.

My dad taught me how to "break in a baseball glove." That's a lost art! Kids today don't know anything about breaking in a glove. First, you had to get some glove oil, or neatsfoot oil, and rub it into your glove. You worked the leather of the glove back and forth until it softened up. Then you got a baseball and put it your glove, wrapped a string around the glove with the ball in it, and slept on it for about a week. My dad could break in a glove in a day. Your glove should be so soft that when you put it down it would just close on it's own.

Every now and then I would watch my dad play. I loved playing, but his team always looked like they were having fun. Real fun! A couple of times I would talk my dad into letting my team play against his team. We were cocky sixteen and seventeen-year-old kids playing against grown men. They always squashed us like grapes. But I couldn't get over how much fun they were having!

The year I turned eighteen, I joined one of my father's teams. It was a bar league. That meant if you lost the game, the losing team had to go to the winning team's bar and spend a certain amount of money. I made the team and played shortstop. My brother Vance joined too, and he played the outfield. This was the greatest time ever! My dad on the mound, me at short, and Vance in left. I remember we won the first game and we all went back to the bar to celebrate...both teams. I got to the bar (back then you could drink at eighteen), and the bartender asked me what I wanted to drink. I had never drank in a real "Man's" bar. Up until then, all I ever had was crappy beer and fruity drinks with my friends when we were sneaking around.

"What'll you have?"
I didn't know what to ask for, so I asked for a drink I had once before.

"I'll have a Singapore Sling!"
You could have heard a pin drop. Who goes to a "Man's" bar and orders a Singapore Sling? With their Dad!
The whole bar erupted into laughter!

"Gene! You teach your boy to drink? You sure you didn't bring your daughter?" Do you think I was embarrassed? I don't think my dad ever heard the end of that! By the end of the night I think I had whiskey, scotch, bourbon, vodka, tequila and I think somebody gave me some moonshine. That was probably the second drunkest day of my life! (The first? My mother had to pull me out of my own vomit in my bed.)

At the end of the night, I got my bicycle out to head home. My dad caught me and made me put my bike in the car and drove me home. Good thing too. I probably would have been the first bicycle DUI.

The next season my dad quit the team and started an umpires' school. He took over all the little leagues and softball leagues in Queens and Manhattan. I quit the team too and became an umpire. You know what I learned? It wasn't about playing softball with my dad, it was just about being with my dad. That was the fun part. Sometimes we would umpire together. I remember once I was the field umpire and I made a bad call in right field. He came out and asked me what happened. I told him how I saw the call. I thought for sure he was going to overturn my call, but he didn't. He backed me up. I'm sure he knew I was wrong, but he never said a word.

My father loved fishing too, and still does. When we were kids we could miss a day of school if we went fishing with him. I hated fishing. But being out there with my dad and my brothers was a great time.

When I had kids I never forgot that. I would take my sons Johnny and Kenny on the road with me. The comedy club I was performing at would put me up in a resort and we'd swim in the pool all night. When we were done, we would go get doughnuts. Sometimes when I had a show at home, my wife would be asleep when I walked in the house, but the kids wouldn't be. We'd sneak out and go to the arcade and play video games. When Kevin Jr. was born, from the time he was six, he would be at my side at every comedy club I'd perform at. It got to the point where I even put him in the show. (Youtube it.) He even did stand-up on his own. He was on a show called "Comedy Kids." (You can still buy it on Amazon.) Sometimes I'd show up at clubs and the first thing people would say to me was, "Where's your son?" That's how close we were. We still are.

I always hear about boys who grow up without a father or a father figure. I think that's an absolute shame. My mother (the psychologist) always tells me how important the father/son dynamic is to a family, especially for raising the next generation of men. I never thought about it much until I had kids. I didn't care about playing softball or fishing, but I loved being with my dad for the day. I'm sure my kids didn't care about going to resorts, or even hanging out at the comedy clubs all night. They just enjoyed our time together.

Although Kevin loved it, and still does!

Anyone can be a father — it takes a whole lot more to be a dad.

# Hide and Seek

My father used to shop at a place called Gouz. It was a dairy farm in Elmont, New York. Their slogan was "Gouz rhymes with cows." It was a dairy farm. Get it?

He'd buy milk, cereal, juice, punch, ice cream, and cookies there. With four kids you have to buy a lot of milk, cereal, juice, ice cream and cookies — and he did. The cereal was the only thing we'd really fight about. We didn't fight about who was going to get it or what kind it was, but who was going to get that prize! The unwritten rule was, "If you were eating the cereal when the prize fell out, it was yours." Sometimes there was no prize, but if you sent two box tops to Battle Creek, Michigan they'd send you a better prize! (I'm still waiting for my baking soda powered submarine!)

My father hated buying cereal because he had to buy so many different kinds. My favorite was Captain Crunch, my brothers liked Rice Krispies and Sugar Pops. You could say "sugar" back then. "Frosted Flakes" were originally "Sugar Frosted Flakes." There were also Sugar Smacks, Sugar Wheats, Sugar Puffs, Sugar Jets, and Sugar Crisps. There was also a weird cereal called "Shredded Wheat." Shredded Wheat is still on the shelves at stores today, but now it's bite sized frosted nuggets. When I was a kid, it came out of the box as a big block of wheat. It was about the size of a small pillow. It was like something you'd give to a horse! It would soak up half a bottle of milk and never even get soft. Yuck!

Every so often my father would try to get slick and buy the big "Variety Pack" of cereal. It was 16 mini boxes of cereals of all different varieties. The coolest thing about the boxes were that they were perforated down the middle of the box, so that you could cut the box open, pour in the milk, and eat the cereal right out the box! Sounds like a great idea, but the technology wasn't created yet to have watertight linings, so when you cut through the center of the box, you usually cut through the entire box. When you would pour the milk in, it would just spill out the box all over the place. Plus, there were always cereals in the variety pack that no one would ever eat, like "Special K." My brothers would try to convince me that "Special K" was a cereal that was just for me because my mother would call me "K." They said that was my "special cereal." Even I wasn't falling for that! Special K was like corn flakes gone bad. No kids ever ate them! I love them now though.

Everything else my father bought he always bought plenty of when he went to the store. The ice cream he bought was this great big tub of ice cream — I mean really big! It could probably double as a bathtub when the ice cream was gone. What flavor? Who cared! It was ice cream! My father would also buy containers of juice for everybody and lots of it! Four kids will go through ice cream, juice, and cookies in a heartbeat, and my father knew that. We had two freezers at my house. One was part of the refrigerator and the other was a freestanding freezer in the basement. Now, my father knew if he went to Gouz on Sunday, all that juice, ice cream, and cookies would be gone by Tuesday, and he'd never get any. So what he used to do was buy us "ice cream" and buy himself *ICE CREAM*. He would buy himself a half-gallon of premium

Breyer's Butter Pecan Ice Cream. Then he would hide it way in the back of the freestanding freezer. We all knew it was there. No one dared touch it either...until about Thursday. Hey! We were kids! By Tuesday we were out of our ice cream; what were we supposed to do? So when nobody was around, you'd get yourself some of his premium ice cream. It was DELICIOUS! Our ice cream barely had flavor. Chocolate tasted like vanilla, strawberry tasted like vanilla, and vanilla? It had no taste at all!

But, Breyer's Butter Pecan Ice Cream? Oh my! It was like frozen heaven! It was sweet, and creamy, and it had whole fresh pecans in it! Why didn't he buy this for us? I'll tell you why. We were kids! You think we would have taken the time to appreciate the great taste of Breyer's Ice Cream? Heck no! We would have scarfed it down and came back looking for more! The only reason we appreciated my father's Breyer's Ice Cream was because it was forbidden fruit. You couldn't take a big scoop of it either because he'd notice that. You had to take just a spoonful, and then smooth out the scoop you just removed. It was wrong, but tasted so right! The one thing you couldn't do was eat it all. So what would happen was, we'd eat it down to the last corner of the container. Then we'd stop.

My father would go to get his ice cream, notice it was almost all gone, and he'd explode! He'd come running upstairs to our rooms, "WHO ATE ALL OF MY ICE CREAM!" Well first, I know he'd be wrong because there was some left — look in the corner of the container! Second, as every kid knows, if he can't prove it, then I didn't do it! My father would go room to room with that container of ice cream like a lawyer showing it to a courtroom jury. "DID YOU DO THAT?" You'd look into that container and say, "No," but what you're thinking is, "Can I have that last bit in the corner?" Then he'd yell at us up and down the hallway, "I BUY ALL THAT ICE CREAM AND CRAP DOWN THERE AND YOU EAT UP MY ICE CREAM!" My mother would be at the bottom of the stairs, yelling up to him, "Just forget it! I did it okay?" I think she would get tired of the yelling and just confess that she did it...or maybe she really did eat it! Go yell at her!

"I SWEAR IF I GET ALL OF YOU OUT OF THE HOUSE AT ONE TIME I'M GOING TO CHANGE THE LOCKS!" (That was his favorite line.)

Now you would think it was just the ice cream. Nope. Anything he bought and hid, we'd find it and eat it. At one point he used to hide a can of cookies under his bed! How crazy is that? But we found them, and we ate them.

In defense of my brothers and sister, I would like to present this evidence to the court. We got ice cream, he got Breyer's Premium Ice Cream. He got Oreo's. We got Hydrox! That was the poor man's excuse for Oreo's. He would also buy himself Chips Ahoy chocolate chip cookies. What did we get? "Chip" Ahoy. Not "Chip*S*" but "Chip." One chip! There would truly be just one chip in every cookie! After we tasted the sweet nectar of the goodies he was eating, how could we go back to that plain wrap crap? We were hooked on the good stuff!

To this day, if you go in my father's bedroom it's stocked with all sorts of goodies. Some habits are hard to break. And we still find them and we eat them.

One day when my kids were in the kitchen I looked in the back of the freezer and noticed my Ben and Jerry's Ice Cream had been opened. I hadn't opened it! I looked inside and there was maybe half a spoonful left. I turned around and none of the kids would look me in the eye.

I knew! They knew I knew! I knew they knew I knew!

I walked over the table and waved that empty container under each one of their noses. "YOU DO THIS? YOU DO THIS?" My wife heard me yelling and came in, "I did it okay? Good lord, it's just ice cream!"

I've never told my father that story. I should, but I won't.

I think he already knows. I know he knows.

# The Big Show

When it comes to kids' holidays, Christmas is numero uno. Rich or poor, Christmas tops the list! Toys, food, toys, family, toys, you get the idea. I'll speak about this more later. Christmas is great, but in my neighborhood, number two on the holiday list was definitely Easter.

Fourth of July was good, but it's summertime and you're already out of school. Who needs a holiday when you're already out of school? What a waste! Thanksgiving was another good one, but back then, you only got four days off. Four days? That just meant more homework! Back in the day, long weekends just meant your teacher gave you more homework because, as they would always say, "You have more time to do it!" (Which was true, but you still waited until the last minute!)

Halloween was a good *day,* but first, you never knew what day it would fall on, so some years you had school the next day. Second, sure you got candy, but you had to go get it! We'd walk miles and miles for the houses that gave out full size candy bars — no bite sized bars like they give out today! Snickers, Payday, and my favorite, Almond Joy! It was like getting two candy bars! Some houses gave out caramel apples, candy apples, or popcorn balls. Looking back, I can really appreciate the time and effort they probably put into making homemade treats, but no kid wants homemade treats! What a jip! Caramel apples and popcorn balls were the worst because they were sticky, and all your good candy would stick to it and get ruined. When you got one of those it was customary to wait a few blocks before you tossed it out of your bag. We always thought it would be cruel if the lady who made them was walking down the street the next morning and saw a pile of popcorn balls and caramel apples blocking the sewer. Candy apples were just as bad — they wouldn't melt, but they made your sack heavy. Plus, every kid had heard the classic urban legend, "My cousin knew a kid who bit into a candy apple and there was a razor blade in it!" First, never in the history of Halloween has a kid ever bit into an apple with a razor blade in it. Second, every urban legend in my neighborhood started with, "My Cousin knows a kid..." As in, "My cousin knows a kid who swallowed a watermelon seed, and a watermelon grew in his stomach." Or "My cousin knows a kid who ate at the Kentucky Fried Chicken on Jamaica Avenue, and bit into a rat." That one is a Jamaica Queens classic! No one ever questioned the validity of any of these claims. We just figured this guy's cousin, "knew a kid." We didn't think of them as *lies*. We had heard them all enough, and they had a ring of truth. Plus, his cousin knows the kid!

Now, you knew a kid in your neighborhood was lying if he said something happened "down south." Just about everyone had relatives that lived down south —Virginia, Georgia, the Carolinas — which they would always go visit in the summer. So when we would hear a kid say, "I saw a girl naked!" We'd say, "No you didn't! Where?" If his response was, "down south!" We all knew that was a lie. For him it was the perfect cover — who could check his details? But no one ever really called you on the "down south" whopper because we all knew we'd have to use it one day. Even if you didn't have relatives down south, you didn't want *your* lie challenged in the court of kid-dom.

The other thing that was a no-no on Halloween was the plastic pumpkin! Only rookie trick or treaters walked around with those. They barely held any candy! You might get two Zagnut bars, a box of Good and Plenty, and a handful of candy corn in one of those things. Tops! Any real kid on candy patrol carried the only thing that a true trick-or-treater would carry. A pillowcase! You could go miles and miles without refilling a pillowcase. I think we walked from Queens, New York to Hartford, Connecticut once with only one refill. We were in a zone!

In my neighborhood there really were no "costumes," per se. There were a few kids dressed as cowboys, or in their old little league uniforms. They were the same kids with the plastic pumpkins! Most of us in my neighborhood were broke. Who was going to ask their parents for money for a costume? So no one got a *real* costume. (I have to say, one year my mom made me a devil costume, with a tail, horns, and a pitched fork! It was the best costume EVER! Thanks Mom!) Every year, just about every kid had the same costume: a ghost. The ghost costume was a simple one. All you had to do was get the sheet off your bed, cut two holes for eyes, and you had a costume. There were all kinds of ghosts patrolling our neighborhoods. Ghosts with stripes, ghost with flowers, fitted ghost, and even ghost with pee stains! It was hard to stand next to a kid with a pee stained ghost sheet on because he would stink! But we would do anything for candy — that trumped all!

Easter? Easter was special. A whole week off of school, coloring Easter eggs, and Easter baskets, which meant MORE candy! Just so you know, nobody likes a hollow chocolate Easter bunny. SOLID milk chocolate is the only way to go. But the crown jewel of Easter, the pièce de résistance, was Easter clothes! Poor, or not, everyone in my neighborhood got Easter clothes. We only got new clothes twice a year. We got them once right before school started, and these were known as "school clothes." The others were Easter clothes.

To break it down, you had play clothes, school clothes, and good clothes. School clothes were just that: clothes you wore to school and only school! You got home, you took those clothes off, you put on your play clothes, and then you went back outside to play. Good clothes were clothes you wore to church, grandma's house, and of course, Easter. Easter clothes weren't like school clothes. School clothes were tough stuff: corduroy, denims, heavy stuff, clothes built to last a school year. (And too big!)

Easter clothes were special. Suits, double breasted, single breasted, pin-stripes, full button down shirts, cuff links, ties, dresses, blouses, socks with frills, hats, shoes — it looked like you just fell out of the pages of the Sears catalogue! (Google it!) We were *CLEAN*! My mother always took my brothers and me to a store in Manhattan called Barney's. Barney's then and now was the top of the food chain when you talk about men's fashion. I never could understand how my mother could afford to take three boys to Barney's every year and buy us suits. I'm a grown man with a great job, and to this day I can't afford to shop at Barney's! I loved going to Barney's. My mother would always ask to be waited on by the manager. Never just one of the salesman, she always wanted the manager. Then we'd stand on a stool in a three-sided mirror and the manager would measure us from head to toe. My mother would call all the shots. Pants length, pleats, cuffs, collar size, jacket size. Everything was custom cut. She'd give us choices, but she was good at steering us into the clothes she wanted us to have. We always got the same thing too: One suit, two extra pairs of pants, which matched the suit, two shirts, that matched the suit, two ties, again that matched the suit, socks, and a pair of black shoes. Those matched everything. When we got home my sister would make us have a "preliminary fashion show." We all had to put on our clothes and walk up and down the hallway and tell each other how "fly" we were! Like I said, this was the "preliminary fashion show," just the practice run before the big event.

Easter day was special. We'd run downstairs, get our baskets, and then go on an Easter egg hunt in the house. My mom, or later my sister would hide eggs all over the house, and then we'd find them. We used real eggs too, not those plastic eggs. So, hopefully we'd find them all. Sometimes we were on our game, we'd find all those eggs in no time flat. That was when my mother would hide them. My sister though hid them as if she was hiding the treasures of the Incas! What was she thinking? The more time we'd spend looking for eggs, the less time we had for our Easter baskets! Usually after about nine eggs we'd give up. My sister always lost track of where she hid them, so she'd just join us on our baskets. Sometime about the middle of April, my father would find those last three eggs. Two-week-old eggs aren't that hard to find. They pretty much jumped out at you! He'd start screaming, "Who put eggs behind the radiator? What is wrong with you stupid kids? There are rotten eggs all over this house!" (That's the clean version.)

Like I said, putting on our Easter clothes and walking up and down the hallway was the "preliminary fashion show."

The "Big Show" was Easter day. Easter day was the biggest neighborhood fashion show anywhere in the world. It was bigger than the famous 5th ave. Easter Day Parade. Here's how it worked. First you took a bath. I say that because there were kids in my neighborhood where "bath" was a four-letter word. Everyone took a bath on Easter! Then you'd slap on your dad's aftershave. My dad wore Canoe for years. One year my brothers and I got our own cologne. I got High Karate! Oh yeah! Next, you put on your clothes very meticulously. We made sure every button was buttoned correctly and every tie was straight. Heaven forbid you button your shirt or jacket incorrectly. You'd lose all your "fly" points.

Now there was only one rule on Easter, and your mom made sure you heard it loud and clear. "Don't Get Dirty!" That was the universal rule in every household and in every neighborhood. Every kid knew it too. There were other days when you were going somewhere special and your mother would say to you, "Don't get dirty," and you'd still go outside to run, or play, but on Easter, that was law! I don't know what the exact punishment was for getting dirty on Easter because NO ONE EVER GOT DIRTY! No one! We had no real idea what would happen. There was no, "My cousin knows a kid" or "When I was down south" for this. No one had ever tested the waters of getting dirty on Easter!

Easter day 1969, it all changed. Everything was off to a great start. We bathed, splashed on some Canoe, and got dressed like every other year. As we headed outside, we heard the mantra, "DON'T GET DIRTY!" "Ok mom!" We headed outside. I felt a chill in the air like none ever before, and I knew something bad was going to happen, but I didn't pay it any mind. I was FLY! My sister would lead us out. She'd walk in front of us like a drum majorette. Our heads were held high, shoulders back, and as sharp and as fly as we could be! I will say this, no one, and I mean no one, was as clean and as fly as the Jordan children on Easter Sunday. We'd walk out of the house and walk right down the middle of the street. The only thing that was missing was Jordan family theme music. We were that fly! First we'd walk to Padden's candy store. We didn't really need anything, but it was a busy street and my sister knew lots of people would see us. Then, we'd walk around the corner and up a block where St. Pascal Church was. If we timed it right, church would just be letting out, and we'd see some of our friends. They could see first hand how fly we were! Then we'd walk home and sit on the stoop. When we sat on the stoop any other day, we'd just sit. Easter was different. We'd put down about four newspapers underneath us so that nothing on us got dirty. If we saw someone coming up the block, we'd jump up and walk right at them and have a "fly-off" challenge. (It was just a face-off of who looked the best. We'd always win.)

Easter day, 1969. It was a beautiful spring day in New York. Every kid in the neighborhood was out in force this day. We were all checking out each other's clothes, sitting on the stoop playing "That's my Car!"

"That's My Car" is played by saying, "That's my car" on the next car that came through the block. Sometimes it would be a nice car and everyone would get all excited, as if it was really your car! Other times a piece of crap car would drive by, and if you said, "That's My Car," you got a "Hunk-a-Junk" and the ridicule that went with it until you called a good car and the pox was off your head.

We were sitting on the stoop and a kid named Mark, who lived around the corner, came and joined us. He was dressed in his fly Easter duds, not as fly as the Jordan kids, but he was okay. The problem was he brought with him the one thing no kid had ever brought outside on Easter Sunday. A Football. Was he crazy? Who was going to play football today? We were all too clean and too fly! Nobody was going to play with that dirty football, besides, he knew the rule, DON'T GET DIRTY! Why would he bring out such a temptation?

At first we all ignored him. But he kept throwing that football in the air and catching it. He wasn't even getting dirty. How could this be? Had we been lied to all these years? Then he threw the ball to my brother Vance. Vance jumped out of the way. He didn't want any part of that ball. Vance was one of the greatest street football players of all time too! I remember my buddy John went over and picked it up and tossed it back to Mark. He caught it with his hands out in front of him, away from his body. No dirt. Wow! He tossed it back to John and John caught it. No dirt on him either! Had we found a loophole in the law? A black hole in the force of the neighborhood? Now everyone was catching the football. It was like a game of hot potato. If someone threw it to you, you either caught it with your hands extended out in front of you, or you got the hell out of the way! We all knew what was at risk. Like with any kids' game, and like all kids, the stakes got cranked up. John threw it to me, I caught it, I threw it to Hopper, it bounced off his hand so he made a backhand catch, and he threw it to Barry who remarkably caught it over his head. And then it happened.

Barry threw it to Mark. It went high and deep. Mark had just witnessed two great catches and couldn't be outdone. Mark turned and dove for the ball. It was probably the greatest catch I'd ever seen. It was straight over his head, as he dove and spun around. He caught it without ever seeing it. It was better than the Super Bowl IX catch by Lynn Swann. It was better than the New York Giants Odel Beckham three-finger touchdown catch. (Google it!) We all went crazy! What a catch! Then it got deathly silent. My sister screamed, "Look!" When Mark got up, he was filthy. He didn't just have dirt on him, he had ground-in street dirt. To top it off, there was a hole in the right knee of his Easter pants suit. You could see it in Mark's face as it hit him too. At first, he had the biggest grin on his face as he stood up. He knew that catch was spectacular, but as he saw our faces, he looked down at his clothes and realized what he had done. He had not only gotten dirty, he had tore his pants. We all ran over to him and tried to wipe the dirt off, but it was no use.

Just then we all heard the one thing no kid wanted to hear. Mark's mother was standing at the end of the block calling him home. We all knew this was the end. My sister broke down and started crying. Mark walked over and handed me the ball. He looked me in the eyes as if to say, "It's ok, I'll see you all later," but as he walked towards his mother, we all knew we'd never see him again. The soft sounds of taps could be heard as he disappeared around the corner, and then we heard what sounded like a car crash and Godzilla. We found out later that was the sound his mother made when she saw what he had done. We never saw

Mark again. We'd see his brother, Pete, but Mark was never seen. Years later Mark's mother had a baby girl. We'd see her walking the baby around the neighborhood, but we never saw Mark. I was always too afraid to ask Pete what happened to his brother. I had always heard the phrase, "grounded for life," but I didn't know if it actually happened. I still have Mark's football. I never played with it after that day. I just don't think it would be right.

From that day, my cousin's could honestly say, "My cousin knew a kid…"

# Summertime

Every summer when my grandkids get out of school I ask them what they're going to do all summer. They always give the same look, "Do? It's summer. We're not going to DO anything!" In fairness, one of my grandkids does play soccer, and he's pretty good too. But after the game, it's right back to "Call of Duty" on the big screen TV. I have another grandson who plays baseball. I think it's baseball. They have uniforms and gloves on, but no one keeps score, they're not allowed to slide, and the ball is soft. Is that baseball?

When we were kids we lived for summer vacation! Today they have Summer break, Spring break, Fall break, Winter Break, and a half day of school every week! When are they in school?

A couple of summers my parents sent me off to camp. Just me. I didn't understand that at all. When they sent Vance and Gene to camp they sent them together, but me they sent alone! I didn't get it. Plus they sent my brothers to a *real* camp. "Camp Wabasaki." It even sounded great. It had horses and cabins and a lake. My mother was working for social services at the time, so she sent me to welfare camp! I don't even think it had a real name. Everyone just called it, "Camp Welfare." It had a pool and cabins, but everyday kids would escape and try to go home. Every morning we had to stand in front of our cabins and do a head count. Sure enough there'd always be three or four kids missing.

We didn't really do crafts like other camps either. I think we were a child labor force for some local factory. We were always making picture frames or pot holders, but they would never let us have them. They'd say, you'll get them when you leave. I'm still waiting! There was no cell phones back then, so the only way to get a hold of your parents was by letter. I think they would go through our mail like a prison because my letters never made it home! I'm sure my mother's reasoning to send me to that camp was, since it was free to send me, why not? Because it was welfare camp, that's why not! To make matters worse, I had this weird feeling that they were sending me to camp so they could secretly move away. I'm sure that never crossed their minds, but that's kid logic for you. Sometimes I would come home from school and just stand in the doorway and yell, "MAAAAAAA!" until she answered. (My kids say I'm a momma's boy. I say, damn straight!)

I hated going away to camp. All the fun was right there on my block and we had everything too! Back then I guess the city was big on social programs. Every other day we'd get some kind of "special truck" that would come through our neighborhood.

We'd get the "Bookmobile." This was like a mobile library. They'd come through your block and give out books to kids.

The "Puppet Truck." This was a truck that would come to the park and put on puppet shows with really elaborate marionettes.

The "Skate Truck." This truck would come to the park and rent out roller skates. Now when I say, "rent out," you had to leave your shoes and they would let you use a pair of skates. That's a fair trade. I'll give you a rundown pair of Pro-Ked sneakers with holes in the bottom and the soles hanging out, and you give me a nice pair of skates. Let's just say that truck only came around once.

One of the craziest trucks that came through was the "Pool Truck." This was a giant truck that had a huge container on the back filled with water! They'd drive that truck all over Queens for kids to swim in, but I don't think they ever changed the water! By the time it got to our block, it was like swimming in swamp water! Think that stopped us? Heck no! We'd dive right in! A few years later they built a pool in the park up the street. There would be so many kids in the pool when you got in you had to stand completely still because there was no room to move. Kids would even bring soap to the pool. Really?

We had other trucks that came through our neighborhood too. The ice cream trucks. Mr. Softee, Bungalo Bar, and Good Humor. They came around once a day, everyday. Bungalow Bar's truck was cool. It was a truck that looked like a house. When the driver stopped the truck, he'd let you climb onboard and ring the bells. He would wear a change maker on his belt (Google it) and make change in lightning speed. I thought that was the coolest thing I'd ever seen. I always wanted one of those things. I still do! Good humor had really good ice cream: Toasted Almond, Bomb Pops, and every Fourth of July they would sell an ice cream called the, "Red, White, and Blueberry." It was just a vanilla ice cream bar covered with red, white, and blue coconut. But since you only could only get it around the Fourth of July that made it special. Marketing genius! Mr. Softee sold soft serve ice cream.

Comedian Eddie Murphy did the greatest comedy routine about the Mr. Softee truck. He talked about how you would hear the truck's song two blocks away, and start running around trying to gather up enough money to buy a "Shaggy Dog" cone or a "Banana Boat" sundae when he came through the block. Then he tells a story about how the driver would just keep driving and make you chase him for blocks until he would stop. (Please Google it; it's hilarious!) You know what all these ice cream trucks have in common? They sold ice cream! You know what the ice cream truck sells that comes through my neighborhood now? Everything BUT ice cream! My sons would ask me for money for the ice cream truck and come back with a water gun or chilli fries. Where's the ice cream?

Summertime was magical in my neighborhood. We'd spend all day outside, even when it rained! We'd get popsicle sticks and race them down the block in the water along the curb to the gutters. Remember collecting popsicle sticks and building a bird house? We didn't need our parents around us 24/7 mapping out our every minute of everyday. We made up things to do.

We had this one game we called, "going on an adventure!" We'd go from my backyard, which was in the middle of the block, all the way to the corner house behind the garages and through the backyards of all our neighbors. Where's the adventure? Well some neighbors didn't want anyone in their yards, some neighbors were in their backyards at the time, and some neighbors had dogs in their yards. It wasn't easy to make it all the way to the corner and back without getting caught! Besides, Mrs. Cramer and Mrs. Richardson were also watching!

Do you know what I used to love to do as a kid? Climb trees. I loved it! The higher and bigger the tree the better. You never see kids climb trees anymore. On the corner of my block lived the Breehm family. They owned a carpet store around the corner. In their yard they had a pear tree. A pear tree in Queens. We'd sneak into his yard and climb that tree to steal pears. I don't even like pears, but secretly poached pears are delicious! I know Mr. Breehm knew we were climbing his tree and stealing his pears. What were we hurting?

I remember once getting into a fistfight with my friend Johnny Morgan. By fistfight, I mean we had our hands balled up in a fist, and we were squared off to fight, but not one single punch was thrown. You know who broke up the fight? The older kids on the block. They knew we were friends, why would they let us fight? Johnny Morgan and I would play, "super hero" all the time. Don't know that game? Tie a towel around your neck and run around the neighborhood solving crimes. We'd also run through a lawn sprinkler or two along the way. Everybody played that game. Instead of fighting crime, now all I see are youtube videos and news segments of kids fighting and the parents standing around encouraging it. Is that what we're teaching our kids now? That's pretty sad.

I used to have an apple tree in my front yard. One day I watched as some kids snuck around to the side of my house and climbed the tree and got some apples. They thought they got away with something terrific.

Good for them.

# Who Da Man?

When my kids were little, every Fourth of July they would drag me to buy fireworks. I hate California fireworks. In California they have "Safe and Sane" fireworks. Safe and Sane fireworks are the biggest waste of money in the history of mankind. They don't do anything! They just fizzle, crackle, whistle, or shower. I want my fireworks to be neither safe nor sane! I want the boom! The bang! The danger of getting your hands blown off! When I was kid, that's all we heard, "You'll blow your hand off!"

My cousin knew a kid named Charles. His nickname was "Lefty." The story was he was playing with some M-80's. In my day, M-80's were considered the A-bomb of home fireworks. It was rumored that four M-80's were equivalent to one stick of dynamite. Anyway, story goes that Charles taped four M-80's together and lit the fuse. As he wound up to throw, it went off in his hand and blew his hand off. Every kid knows when you throw fireworks you don't take the time to wind up — you toss it right away! My cousin said that when they found Charles' hand it was three blocks away with the lighter still in it. Did I mention Charles lived down south?

Every fourth of July my kids would drag me to some makeshift shack in a supermarket parking lot that was supporting a little league or some other charity, and make me shell out hundreds of dollars on some wanna-be-fireworks. Flowering Fountains, Rainbow Rays, Sparklers, and Piccolo Petes. My nephew had figured out how to plug an empty two-liter soda bottle with a Piccolo Pete and produce a loud explosion. That's as close as we would get to *proper* fireworks.

In my neighborhood, we had REAL fireworks! Nobody wasted their time on "Snakes" and "Sparklers;" those were for babies. We had Firecrackers, Ash Cans, Cherry Bombs, Smoke Bombs, Roman Candles, Bottle Rockets, Sky Rockets, and M-80's! The problem was they were illegal, so where could we buy them? Nobody set up a shack for charity on my block. Every year around the middle of June, some kid from some other neighborhood would pop up and sell some stuff. Maybe some firecrackers, every now and then a bottle rocket or two. We never had a firework dealer in our neighborhood. To get really good fireworks you had to go to Chinatown in Manhattan.

First, to think that you could get from Queens to Manhattan and back with bags of fireworks on the bus and train without getting stopped by the police was impossible. Also, we had always heard that if you went to Chinatown and bought fireworks, after you bought them and left the shop, they would send a guy after you, beat you up with Karate before you got to the subway station, take all your money and the stuff back that they just sold you. My cousin knew a guy…

I tried my hand at selling other things on my block. I used to sell lollipops from my house to the kids in my neighborhood. What I would do was go to Padden's candy store. Mrs. Padden was an old woman who owned a candy store on Farmers Boulevard two blocks from my house. I'd go in and ask her for one hundred lollipops. If she wasn't too busy she'd start counting out lollipops one at a time. One, two, three — I'd let her get to about eighty, and then

I'd say, "Make it two hundred!" She'd get so angry, she'd just start grabbing handfuls of lollipops and putting them in the bag. She'd put about 220-230 lollipops in there. I could sell them at a penny and still make a profit. Then she started catching on to my scheme. Lollipops came 120 to a box, so when I'd ask for 100, she'd just count out 20 and give me the box. For awhile it actually worked out better because I had to raise my prices to two-cents and my profit margin went up. The problem was, kids figured why pay two cents for a pop that costs one cent? Business fell off quick.

When I was in 7th grade I had a friend named Mitchell. Mitchell had the coolest hair I'd ever seen! He was like a thirteen-year-old Fabio! It was the end of May so there was nothing left for us to do in school except wait for school to be over. One day Mitch brought a whole pack of firecrackers to school. TO SCHOOL! That was unheard of in my day! Today kids bring guns and drugs, and no one bats an eye! This was just a pack of firecrackers! I asked him where he got the firecrackers, and he told me his dad was selling them. The wheels in my head started turning. Mitch lived near the school, I could ride my bike to his house, buy some fireworks, and sell them in my neighborhood! That afternoon I went to Mitch's house. His dad had everything! I bought everything I could carry and got back on my bike. Mitch's father would give me "The Speech" every time before I left his house.

"If the police stop you, you tell them you bought these fireworks off a guy in a van, you got that?"

I felt like Ray Liotta in Goodfellas! I was picking up product in one neighborhood and selling in my own neighborhood. Word spread fast that I was selling fireworks, and I had *everything*! Rockets, Blasters, Smoke Bombs, even the highly dangerous, but highly profitable M-80! I was in the firework business, and business was GOOD! I was making more money than I could handle. I was the "Don" of 113th road. I was making runs to Mitch's house twice a week! Some of the older guys on my block were trying to muscle me too. They'd ask me, "Where you getting your supply?" I'd say, "Off a guy in a van!"

One of my brother's friends, Darryl tried to move in on my territory, but I was moving so much product that I just lowered my prices until I had him buying from me! Heck, now I was a supplier! Kids all over Queens knew me as, "the fireworks boy." I'd be walking down the street and I'd hear, "There's the fireworks boy or sometimes they'd call out to me, "Hey fireworks boy!" I'd just walk along like a king walking through his kingdom. Sometimes kids would come up to me and say, "Hey fireworks boy, can I buy some firecrackers?" I'd ask them, "How old are you?" If he'd say, "I'm 9 years old," I'd look him over and say, "Get lost! I don't sell to little kids. You'll blow your hand off!" (I was only 12!) Even in the firework business you had to have morals!

Like they said in the movie Scarface, "The world is yours!" Indeed it was! I was doing so well, I'd take my friends to New York Mets games, I'd have popcorn and Kool-aid parties in my backyard, hell, when the ice cream truck would come around, I'd buy every kid out there ice cream! Business was booming. I was the king of an empire! But then I got cocky. It was getting close to the Fourth and I had a lot of product to move. I started breaking the cardinal rule. "Don't sell to little kids!" I had no problem with little kids using fireworks — what did I care? You want to blow your hand off, that's fine with me! My cousin already knew a kid! The problem was, little kids are snitches! If you tell a little kid, "Don't tell anybody where you bought this," you can bet your bottom dollar he's going to run and tell the first person he sees where he bought it. The other problem with little kids was they never had enough money! They'd want a pack of firecrackers that would cost twenty-five cents. They'd show up with fifteen cents and want to bargain with you! "NO! Twenty-five cents!" Then they'd come back with twenty-cents! "Didn't I say twenty-five!?" Off they'd go, and back they'd come, "This ain't Twenty-Five! This is Twenty-cents and two marbles!"

My empire was flourishing! The Fourth was a couple of days away, and I had half of Queens under my reign. What could go wrong? One afternoon there was a knock at my door. I could see from the upstairs window it was a, LITTLE KID! What the heck could he want? I ran to the door just as my father opened it. "Can I help you?" The kid says, "Does the fireworks boy live here?" "Firework boy?" My father looked at me like a federal agent catching a drug kingpin! "You selling fireworks?" I WAS CAUGHT! BUSTED! NABBED! STUPID LITTLE KID! He took down the whole 'fireworks boy' empire! My father went into my room, and I showed him my supply. Stashed under my bed were enough fireworks to rival any Disneyland display. He said, "Where did you get all of this?" What could I say? "From a guy in a van!" Hey! I'm nobody's snitch! My father made me dump all the fireworks in the garbage. I told my buddies to get them out of the cans on garbage pick up day and hide them at their house. On the Fourth of July, we set them off ourselves. It was the greatest firework display 113th Road had ever seen. And nobody lost a hand.

My father never lets me forget the summer of "The Fireworks Boy." The funny thing was, he didn't even punish me for that. Deep down I think he was kind of amazed that I had created this little empire at twelve years old, albeit an ILLEGAL EMPIRE! I think he always knew I'd end up working for myself one day in some capacity, he just didn't know what I'd be doing.

At least this time it's legal!

People always ask me, "Where do you get your jokes?" From a guy in a van!

# Kids' Table

If you want to know what your status is in your family hierarchy, all you have to do is go to a Thanksgiving dinner. This is where you'll find out whether your opinions and perspectives are considered childish or adult worthy.

Thanksgiving was always held at my grandmother's house. She lived in a two-bedroom apartment in the Bronx with a doorman and a miniature golf course out in front of the building. Try finding that in the Bronx today! My grandmother wasn't a "pinch your cheek" type of grandma. She was elegant! I remember at my sister's cotillion my grandmother showed up with a beautiful mink stole on. She had a full-length mink coat too. I had never seen a woman with a mink before. The only women who wore minks were rich women in the movies. She looked so regal!

On Thanksgiving everyone would show up at her apartment. Nowadays, when family shows up for Thanksgiving they bring a dish. I don't know if it's to show off your cooking skills or just to help out the person hosting Thanksgiving dinner, but no one dared bring a dish to my grandmothers house! I don't think there was any dish you could bring that was going outshine what she was cooking!

Back then the kids stayed in one room, and the adults stayed in another. Kids weren't allowed to be with adults because they were talking grownup talk. Children knew their place. We would run all over my grandma's apartment — even out on the balcony, but you stayed out of the living room. That was only for adults.

Today, I see kids not only sitting in with their parents when it's just the adults around, but they're joining in on the conversation! A twelve-year-old has an opinion? My mother likes to say that kids are smarter today and they know more. They're exposed to worldly events at an earlier age than we were. So kids today don't like, "kid talk" because it is boring and uneventful. "Adult talk" is exciting and stimulating! I don't know if I totally agree with that. Kids shouldn't be in "grown folks business." That's one old school rule I totally agree with. Nobody wants kids around when you're talking "grown folk" talk. Go play video games. Or better yet, go outside and play!

When dinner was ready everybody had one of two spots to sit at. The adults' table or the kids' table. There were only two ways to get up to the adult table: waiting for someone to die, and lets face it, that's a little awkward. You can't be wishing bad things on your drunk uncle Lou! The other way was graduating up to the adult table, which is even tougher. First you have older cousins in line ahead of you, and then you have your own siblings ahead of you. When they move up, they usually have a spouse that gets a seat with them, so that just sets you further back in the rotation! I was forty-seven when I got the call up to the adult table. I felt like George Jefferson! I was movin' on up! Getting my turn in the big league! Finally. I had stories to tell, tales to share, problems to solve! I had made it!

Just as dinner was about to be served my drunk uncle Lou showed up with his new wife. What's the old adage? Last one in, first one out. So I returned to the kids' table, where food was cut into little pieces and picking your nose is acceptable. I have a dream that one day I too will sit at the adults' table. I'll sit up straight without anyone telling me to do so, and I'll cough and cover my mouth without being prompted. I'll get to say things like, "Please pass the salt," and "This stuffing is delicious!" Someone will ask my opinion, and I will tell them a story that will have then sitting on the edge of their seats! I'll tell a tale that'll weave into a breath taking yarn so incredible that it not only solves their problems, but it'll also solve global warming, AND world hunger at the same time! Those will be my contributions to America, the world, and the adults' table!

Like I mentioned, I cook Thanksgiving dinner for my family. From the turkey to the dessert. I never make apple pie because it just wouldn't be right trying to duplicate my mother-in-law's pie. Can't be done. My son has now started making apple pies for our family holiday get together. And it's very, very good, but it is not my mother-in-law's apple pie!

I learned by watching and doing. My mother would make us stir, beat, baste, knead, mix, sauté, or anything else that had to be done in the kitchen. Sometimes I didn't want to, but as I look back, I'm sure glad I did. My father makes a great chicken and dumplings, and sausage and peppers. I asked him for the recipe, and I wrote it down. My mother makes a great mac and cheese. I asked her for the recipe, and I wrote it down. Everyone should write down the recipes, creations, or anything else they cherish from their parents. Pass it along to your children. Let (and make) your children help you in the kitchen and other things around the house. Everyone will benefit from it. Trust me.

Two side stories:

Side story one - When I first got married, a few days before Thanksgiving you would have to bring a pie dish to my mother-in-law's house. In the beginning I didn't know why. "A pie dish? For what?" Turns out if you brought a pie dish to her house before Thanksgiving, she'd bake you an apple pie that you could take home with you. I remember thinking, "I can bake a pie myself, why do I need her pie?" That's what I was thinking BEFORE I tasted her pie. My mother in law's apple pie would put Marie Callender's to shame! After that first Thanksgiving with my mother-in-law, I brought five pie plates to her house every year! She'd make those pies for us and they wouldn't last a week. That's how good they were! No one can replicate her recipe.

Side story two - My buddy Ron told me that when he got married his wife's family had this crazy Thanksgiving tradition. His wife had two sisters also. Every Thanksgiving they would have the dinner at either his house, one of the two sisters' houses, or his mother-in-law's house. They would all bring a dish, and whoever's house it was would make the turkey. Then on the Friday after Thanksgiving they would take all the side dishes to another one's house and that person would make a turkey and would have a Friday Thanksgiving there. THEN on Saturday, they would again take all the side dishes (or make more if necessary) to another sister's or mother's house, THAT person would make a turkey, and they'd have Thanksgiving dinner again. Then on Sunday — you guessed it! They'd do it all over again at the last person's house.

Ron said they would do this every year, year after year, eating the same dishes with the same people, all sitting in the same exact spots! He said it was the craziest thing he ever witnessed! He finally told his wife, "Pick one day, and that's the dinner I'm going to. I'm not going to everybody's house all weekend long!" He said his wife would yell and scream at him to go with her, and he would just wait for the party to come to his house because he knew one of those four days it would with the same people, and the same food! He told me his wife was so angry that she had her father talk to him. He said his father-in-law told him he was so proud of Ron for being brave enough to stop coming to these awful weekend-long dinners, and he wished he had the guts to do what Ron was doing! Ron got a divorce a year later.

Dr. Phil always asks couples, "Do you want to be right? Or do you want to be happy?"

Ron was both.

# Best Day Ever!

No day was ever better than Christmas. Ever! Actually, Christmas Day wasn't even as exciting as the time leading up to Christmas. Every year right after Thanksgiving (now they start Christmas shopping the day after Labor day), Sears and Robuck would put out their Sears Catalogue "Wish Book." It was a catalogue of all their products they sold at the store, but at Christmas time, it was full of every toy imaginable. The other catalogue, which was even better than Sears, was the Spiegel catalogue. It was equally as enticing, but it was better because it had a much bigger selection. We read those catalogues like the Pope reading the bible. "I want this!" "I'm getting that!" We'd circle and cut out everything in that catalogue. To their credit, my parents did their best to make every wish come true. (Thanks!) Although, I will say, I asked for "Rock-em, Sock-em Robots" and never got them! I used to talk about that in my comedy act, and when I turned 50, my mother sent me those "Rock-em, Sock-em Robots!" I guess after all these years my mother just couldn't stand the guilt. My son, since he was ten, has been asking me for this drone you can fly with your iPhone that he saw at a Brookstone store. He'll get it when he's 50.

Here's where I really feel sorry for kids today. I asked my niece and nephew what they wanted for Christmas. They said they wanted gift cards. They didn't want a toy or anything they could play with that day. They both wanted a gift card. Why a gift card? So they could go buy what they wanted to get! Hey, geniuses! THAT'S WHAT I WAS GOING TO DO! Their mother explained to me that with a gift card they could go on the Internet and buy things for the games they were playing online. That is sickening. Why even wake up Christmas morning? Where's the excitement? The anticipation?

I remember we weren't allowed to come downstairs until a certain time. My sister was the timekeeper. We'd all wake up and meet in her room. Then when the time came, we'd run downstairs and see piles of toys. GIANT PILES! It looked like a toy store explosion! Who wants to run downstairs to a gift card? Kids today don't know the phrase, "some assembly required," or "batteries not included." Every toy we got said that! All the toys and games today require no imagination. That's sad.

I remember having Tonka trucks. They were made of steel! They used to have a commercial where an elephant would stand on a Tonka truck. They were that strong. They were no match for the Jordan boys, but they were tough.

Hey, remember this game? You'd get your GI Joes, and they go over to your sister's Barbie's Dream House, beat up Ken, and take Barbie away in her Corvette? Everybody played that game!

All my friends today play Madden Football. I have to admit, it's a great game, but was there any game better than electric football? (Google it!) We had an entire electric football league in my neighborhood. I had the Pittsburgh Steelers. (I still have them to this day!) My sister had a Suzy Homemaker Easy-Bake Oven. It would bake a cake about three inches in diameter, and it had a box of frosting too! No kid should ever get a toy called Lite-Brite. Oh sure we started out making a flower or a clown's face, but then what did we all do? We would write neon lighted dirty words!

My greatest Christmas ever? One year my parents bought all our toys through the Spiegel catalogue. Two days before Christmas they started panicking because the toys hadn't arrived yet. This is before Fedex, Amazon or package tracking, so they went out to stores and bought every toy again just to be sure. The day before Christmas all the toys showed up. It was too late to take everything back, so they just let us have EVERYTHING! We had two of every toy we asked for. What a day!

Christmas vacation was great because you got a week off from school. One week. Now they get a month and you have to call it "Winter Break" because saying "Christmas" is not allowed! We usually got homework too! How crazy is that? Even the smart kids didn't do Christmas homework!

The two biggest gifts you could get at Christmas was a bike, or a sled. What was the best bike to get? A Schwinn, Royce Union, Pierce Arrow, Tour De France? All great choices. However, when it came to sleds, there was only one choice. The Flexible Flyer. It was the best sled on the market! The Maserati of sleds. The G7 of the snow, the…you get it. It was the best sled EVER! But no on ever got one. We had all heard of it, and had seen it in the Spiegel catalogue, but no had ever seen one in person. My friend said he had a cousin down south that had one. You had to believe it. No one ever asked for a sled for Christmas. If you get a sled, you need snow. I can ride a bike in any weather, rain, cold, even snow! But a sled?

Who wanted to waste a request on a gift that was so limited?

The only day better in the winter than Christmas Day was a snow day! Usually in January or February we'd get a blizzard in New York. Now, you would think that a blizzard meant that all schools were automatically closed, as they would do today. No way! There'd be eight or nine inches of snow on the ground, and you still dressed as if you were going to school. Before they had 24-hour news, and before the Internet, there was the radio. All local news was found out on the radio. When it snowed, every radio station would tell you what schools were closed due to the weather. If your school wasn't called, your parents would send you out the door with your boots, scarf, hat, sweater, and your winter coat. All mothers back then used to smear Vaseline on our faces, about an inch thick. That was supposed to keep us warmer. That's my theory of why "black don't crack." An inch of Vaseline on your skin will preserve you for years!

As we got dressed for school we constantly listened for our school to be called. We'd dress as slow as we could too! Then it would start! "The following schools are closed due to the storm. PS 115, PS 140, PS 235. And then it came, "And PS 118!" It was like the lottery for kids! SNOW DAY! Hot Damn! You could hear the entire neighborhood erupt in joy. What to do first? Snowman? Make a snow angel? Snowball fight with the kids on 194th street? (The kids on that block sucked!) No sooner than our joy was at it's zenith, my father would slap us back into reality. "When you get dressed, go outside and shovel the driveway." I hated shoveling snow! Anyone who's ever had to shovel snow knows that snow is heavy! It's hard work! Shoveling snow is the number one cause for heart attack! A fact my father didn't really care about since he wasn't really worried about three pre-teen boys falling over from a heart attack.

There were no snow blowers back then, plus my father didn't have snow shovels. Snow shovels are lightweight aluminum shovels to offset the weight of the snow. No. My father only had heavy dirt shovels. We didn't have a big yard, but when you're shoveling snow, it was like shoveling the Ponderosa. The worst part was, just as we were finishing, like clockwork, someone would call our house, "Mr. Jordan, can you send your boys over to shovel my yard?" Now most kids made money shoveling snow out of other peoples' yards, but not us. We had to go shovel peoples' yards *for free*! My father would tell us, "Go shovel Mrs. Ross' yard, and don't take any money from her." WHAT? Don't take any money? Who works for free? The Jordan boys that's who! Everybody on our block would call too! Even Mrs. Richardson! Was she kidding? Treat us like crap all summer and want us to shovel her yard in the winter? How rude was that!

My job after we shoveled was to put rock salt on the steps out in front of the house so people wouldn't slip on the ice. My brother would always tell me to skip the salt at Mrs. Richardson's house. I hated her, but I knew I'd feel guilty at the sight of her sliding down those steps because I didn't salt them. So I always did. The rudest part of it all was after we were finished shoveling all that snow, backyard to front yard, across the front of their house and salted their steps, they offered us…a dollar! Not a dollar a piece. One dollar for the three of us! Thirty-three cents a piece! Who works for thirty-three cents? The Jordan boys, that's who! And we couldn't even take that!

For those of you who don't know, when you're a kid, there are two kinds of snow. Bad snow, and good snow. Bad snow is light and doesn't "stick" when you pick it up. Good snow is heavy, thick snow. When you grab a handful of it, it forms right away. My sister had an uncanny knack of knowing good snow from bad snow before it hit the ground. As it snowed she'd taste the snow and she could tell us what kind of snow it was going to be. She was like the "Snow-Whisperer!" Snow days with good snow meant only two things. Snowball fights and the big sled race!

Every snowball fight started the same way. One kid from one neighborhood would throw a snowball at a kid from another neighborhood, then another would join, then another, another, and before you knew it, there'd be hundreds of kids lined up across the street from each other throwing snowballs! There were rules. Rule one was no ice balls. An ice ball is a snowball dipped in a puddle so it freezes. They hurt like hell! Second rule was if a bus comes down the street, everybody throws at the bus. I don't know why we did that, but it was the rule!

We didn't have the high-tech gloves they have today. Our gloves were wool. So after about four or five throws your hands were freezing. Some kids had "pleather" gloves. These were gloves that looked like leather, but were really plastic. But they weren't much better. After your gloves got wet, and your hands were numb, you'd go in the house and get a pair of socks and put them on your hands. Anything was better than nothing.

113th road, where I lived, was a quiet street. One block over was Murdock Avenue, and at the end of the block was Farmer's Boulevard. Both were major streets with a lot of traffic. When the snowplows would come and clear the streets, they would plow Murdock Avenue, and then make a right turn to do Farmer's. However, the plows would push all the snow to one side causing a wall of snow blocking our street. This meant no cars could get in OR out! It was perfect for kids with a day off! The 113th road sled race was legendary. Kids would come from all over to race. The racecourse was simple. We started on 194$^{th}$ street on top of the hill. You ran until the first tree, jumped on your sled, slid down the hill, made a left hand turn on 113$^{th}$, and glided half way down the block to the finish.

Both my brothers and my sister had won the race years before me. February of 1970 was my year. Why? Because six weeks earlier I got the greatest Christmas gift EVER! (Until Christmas of 1971.) Christmas of 1970 I got a Flexible Flyer Sled! It was beautiful! It was a wooden sled polished to a high shine. It had the words "Flexible Flyer" on the boards with an eagle running the length of the sled. On the bottom it had two beautiful red runners on each side. It was truly a sled to behold! Problem was this Christmas day it was sixty degrees outside and sunny! What the heck was I going to do with a sled? Even if it was the legendary Flexible Flyer? It was customary in my neighborhood to go house to house and see everybody's toys. When you get a sled on a sunny winter day everybody looks at you with disappointment. "A sled huh? Man Kev, that's too bad. I feel sorry you!" What could I do? I had to wait. But six weeks later I got my payoff. When I saw everybody heading for the hill for the great sled race, I knew my time had come.

There were two keys to winning. One, you must get a good start. Any Olympic bobsledder will tell you that. Two, you have to make clean turns — no tail slide, and no spin. Clean. As I walked up the hill I could see heads turn as I walked by with my Flexible Flyer. It glistened in the sunlight. No one in my neighborhood had ever seen one. It was like I was moving in slow motion as I heard the ooh's and ahh's as I walked by. They all knew I meant business this year. At the top of the hill was Black Tyrone. Tyrone was, well, black. Jet black. He was our age but he was big. Really, really big. Tyrone always had an afro pick sticking out of his hair and smoked unfiltered cigarettes. Rumor was he had two kids, and could drive. I knew he'd be my only true competition on this day.

"Somebody's daddy got a job and bought his boy a sled!" Every competition in my neighborhood started with "Snaps" or "playing the dozens." (Google it!) Black Tyrone was good at it too. I snapped back, "If you knew who your daddy was, you'd get one too!" Oh snap! Damn! I was on fire! I was ready. I could see the newbie's at the race. Kids with the string dangling from the front of their sleds; that's for pulling your kid sister down the street. They just slow you down when you're racing. Kids with boots on — you can't run in boots! I had on my PF Flyers that day! Sneakers with the action wedge to make you run faster and jump higher! That's what the commercial told us! (Google it!)

I still remember the lineup for the race:
Black Tyrone, John Smith, Horace McDougal, Barry Paige, Smoot, two kids from parts unknown, and me. "Hey, Horace, this ain't the circus. No midgets allowed!"

Like I said, Tyrone was good at "Snappin'" and he knew it would throw everybody off their game. But not me. Not today! "After this race, tell yo momma I'm coming over for dinner!" Horace wasn't really good at "Snappin'." "Horace, yo momma is like the F train; you can ride her all day for thirty-five cents!" "OOOHHHHH." The crowd was into it today and Tyrone meant business.

"Yo Kev! Know what's written on the back of my sled?"

"What?"

"You gonna find out!" Dang! How could I walk into that one? I looked over at my brother Gene. He was giving me the "focus" stare. Tyrone took one last drag on his cigarette and crushed it out in the snow. He was 12? Then we lined up at the start.

"On your mark. Get set. GO!

We all bolted from the gate. Everybody was slipping and sliding getting started. It looked like a cartoon with all the legs spinning and no one going anywhere. We were neck and neck as we got to the "jump" tree. This is where you had to jump on your sled. When I left my feet it felt like I propelled myself 10 feet in the air and 20 yards down the hill. I was flying! As I hit the ground I could see Tyrone just out in front of me. I pull myself up on my sled to get more weight on the front. The pack was tight going down the hill. I was gaining on Tyrone as we came up on the turn. This was crucial. I've seen many guys wipeout trying to take the turn too fast. The trick was to drag your foot as a brake just a little so the sled would turn cleaner. Just as we hit the turn, Horace's sled cut inside me, but I could see he was dragging the wrong foot. He was dragging his right foot for a left turn. Rookie mistake! Then it happened.

Horace's foot caught another kid's pull rope and the two of them flipped right over the top of me! I knew if I slowed down they would crash into me. I raised my foot and turned hard with no brake! I had always heard that the flexible flyer was the best cornering sled on the streets, and I was about to put it to the test. Horace crashed into some garbage cans on the curb. There was a big explosion and he took out three kids with him like bowling pins. I was neck and neck with Tyrone as we came out of the turn. I could see and smell his cigarette breath as we whizzed down the street. I started pulling out in front when Tyrone bumped my sled to knock me off. We had fifty yards to go, and again he bumped me, almost knocking me completely off my sled. Now he was right on my side. I could see him nudging his sled to finish me off. I turned my sled back into him. We were tangled together as we approached the finish line. I looked ahead and saw we were heading straight over a manhole cover.

Anybody who lives in the city knows manhole covers don't freeze. Hitting one of those is like running over a patch of cement. I veered right and looked at Tyrone. He was laughing cause he thought I gave up. He never saw the manhole cover. His sled hit the metal cover and he stopped on a dime throwing Tyrone head over heels. I slid across the finish line sideways with a little flare. My brother Vance picked me up off my sled and gave me a hug. I think it was the first time he was truly proud of me.

Ask anyone from St. Albans, New York about the great sled race of 1970, and they'll tell you it was the greatest race of all time. My Flexible Flyer is still hanging in my father garage too.

You don't get that from a gift card.

# First Day-Last Day

They say there's only two good days when you by a boat: the day you buy it and the day you sell it. School is the same exact way. The two most exciting days are the first day of school and the last day of school. Every other day is just a blur. The last day of school is great for the obvious reason: school's out! Summer begins! In retrospect, most of us "checked out" somewhere around the month before school officially let out. Every year we got out of school June 30th, so come May 31st there was nothing you could do, say, or show us that was going to sink into our brains. It was 30 days and counting until school's over! The sun was warm, the days were long, and attention spans were short. Our minds were a million miles away. God bless anyone who is a teacher! You will always have my absolute respect and undying appreciation. You have a truly under appreciated job!

On the last day of school there were a few traditions for us. One, we would open the back door of the school bus and jump out. I don't know why, but we felt like such "bad boys" when we did this. The bus driver never said a word either. The bus ride to and from school by itself was an adventure. Back then there were no real rules on safety. We would sit two-to-three to a seat, and if there weren't enough seats for everybody, some kids would have to stand. How crazy is that? I thank god no one ever got hurt from an accident. The back of the bus was the best place to sit. There was a pecking order to sitting on the bus too. The higher grade you were in, the closer to the back of the bus you got to sit. All the good stuff happened in the back. "Yo Momma" joke fights, or "Snaps."

All the best fistfights were in the back of the bus too. I got into a classic fight with a kid when I was in the fourth grade. This kid was tall! We were wrestling around pretty good, and then I heard my brother Vance yell, "Turn his head this way!" I pushed his face towards my brother and he punched him square in the eye. I've never seen a person's eye swell up so fast right in front of me. It was like watching a cake rise in fast motion. I stood over the kid like I had done something. "You want some more? Huh? You had enough?" I think just about every fight I was in, one of my brothers was standing over my shoulder. You know those cartoons where everybody is afraid of the little dog because the big dog is standing right behind him? That was me.

One of the other games we would play on the bus was called "Bounce." What we would do was bounce up and down in our seats, and when the bus hit a pothole, the whole bus would bounce in the air throwing us all over the bus. Of course the further the back you are in the bus, the higher you get launched. Driving a bus on New York City streets, there were potholes everywhere. You'd have kids flying so high they hit their heads on the roof of the bus!

We had the same bus driver from the time I was in third grade until I was in sixth grade. Amazingly, the bus driver never said a word to us. All the fights and screaming, he never once scolded us or said we were out of control. In fact, I think he enjoyed hitting those potholes in the street and sending us flying head over heels all over the bus.

The only day he ever said anything to us was one day when I was in fourth grade. I remember getting on the bus and it was eerily quiet — too quiet for a school bus full of children going to school. As we boarded the bus, the driver said to us in his thick Jamaican accent, "Our father was killed today, I do not want to hear a word from anyone." I had no idea what he was talking about. My father wasn't killed. I remember going to school and not a word was said about it. No teacher mentioned it, not the principal, no one. I got home that day and watched on the news with my family. Dr. Martin Luther King Jr. had been assassinated. I guess kids today have it better that they get news almost instantaneously. Sometimes they get news before it becomes news. Sad part is, news to them is Snookie from the TV show The Jersey Shore is pregnant, which is somehow more important than the President's State of the Union Address.

The other last day of school tradition was to tie the laces of your sneakers together and then throw them up on to the telephone wire that ran up the street. There'd be 50-60 pairs of sneakers up on the telephone line. The trick was to do it on one throw! You could throw it a second time, but you were really good if could you get them up there in one throw. I told this story to my son and he asked me, "So you walked home in your socks?" (KIDS!) Back then you didn't wear sneakers to school. Sneakers weren't (and aren't) shoes! Everyone wore shoes, and I mean real shoes to school. Hush Puppies, Buster Browns, lace-ups, loafers, and you carried your sneakers in your book bag. You usually had gym twice a week. If you had gym on a Friday at 2 P.M., that was the perfect time because school ended at 3 P.M., so you didn't have to put your shoes back on.

At my school you also would have a day called "Assembly," where boys had to wear a white shirt with dark pants (no one wore jeans) and a tie. Girls had to wear a white blouse and a dark skirt. There would be a color guard that would open the ceremony, and then we'd usually sing songs or see a movie. Sometimes we'd get sales pitches. The 4H club would come once a year and recruit us like they were recruiting for the military. 4H is a farming and agricultural organization. They would show us pictures of kids riding horses, milking cows, and growing corn or sheering sheep. We lived in Queens, New York! It was not your typical farmland! Ever see a cornfield in Queens? Plus the neighbors get a little upset when you try to sheer their dog like a sheep!

The first day of school was exciting! New teacher, new classroom, new grade, but same classmates. Back in the day, for some reason, when you moved from grade to grade, the same kids always stayed together. They used to do it according to proficiency exams. If a kid was an 80% student, they'd put you in with other 80% students. So you may have been the smartest in your class, but you're really only the top of your group, and not really smartest overall. It was like being the smartest dumb kid. Now they don't break kids up because they say it would be bad for their self-esteem. They don't leave kids back a grade for the same reason. They just keep pushing them forward until they're so far behind they can never catch up.

The first day of school meant all new things too. We always got new book bags (backpacks weren't fashionable yet) and new lunch boxes. Every lunch box was made of steel with a thermos inside. The thermos had a glass lining...GLASS! So when (not if), you dropped it, the glass lining would break and that would be the end of your thermos. After that your mother would put a soda in your lunch box and wrap it in aluminum foil. That was supposed to keep it cold. "Supposed to." It never worked. Most lunch boxes back then were based on cartoons. The coolest lunch box I ever had was a Speed Racer lunch box. It came with little magnetic cars, a magnetic spinner, and a racetrack on the backside. THAT WAS COOL! We would all break out our new school threads the first week. Everyone was clean and color coordinated. We'd all get just enough clothes to go a week without repeating, and after that week nobody even cared anymore. The really cool thing was you'd get new shoes. REAL shoes! I hate when I hear kids call sneakers "shoes." They're not "shoes," they're SNEAKERS! (A note from the editor: Technically they are shoes, as sneakers are a form of shoes…signed, my Stanford graduate son.)

When you got new shoes, your mom would get "taps" put on them. Taps were small triangular metal protectors that went on the toe and outer heel of your shoes to keep them from wearing out. They would make a "clicking-clacking" sound when you walked; in fact they were almost like tap shoes that dancers wear. (It was probably where the name came from. Duh!) But here's the best part. The first day of school they would wax the floors of the school to a high polish shine. The floors were so polished in fact that you could run down the hallways and slide on your taps like an ice skater! We would slide up and down the halls on the first day like Bobby Hull the hockey player. You could only do it on the first day. After that, the floors were too dirty and scuffed up from all kids sliding up and down the halls.

Every time my son would tell me he needed new shoes for school (four-to-five times a year BTW!) I would just cringe. They're not shoes! They're SNEAKERS! One hundred dollar sneakers at that! You can't put taps on sneakers. You can't spit-polish sneakers. They're Sneakers!

Buster Brown shoes had a jingle: "Here's Buster Brown! He lives in a shoe! There's his dog Tige, He lives in there too!"

There's no song for sneakers. And you can't slide up and down a hallway.

The first day of school was like a reunion party. We would all catch up with friends you haven't seen all summer, brag about all the things we did over the summer, and check out the new kids. There were always new kids every year. The girl "new kid?" Who cared? Girls had cooties. The boy "new kid" had to be tested. There were two ways to test a new kid. One was seeing how fast he was. For some reason being fast equaled being cool. Every game we played was a running game, so if a kid was fast you wanted him on your team. The other way to test the "new kid" was to see how tough he was. There were more fights on the first day than any other day. We usually knew who the toughest kid in the class was, so he never had to fight the "new kid." It was usually some underling trying to improve his reputation for the year. The sad part was, if the "new kid" beat him down, he slid further back into the pecking order. On the first day of school all pecking orders had to be established!

Cool teachers on the first day let you sit wherever you wanted to, and there wasn't a seat far enough in the back for me! Smart teachers *placed* you in your seats. We hated that! Sit next to a girl for the year? That wasn't going to happen. Amazingly, even when a teacher placed you in seats, less than a month in we were all in different seats anyway. I don't know why they would even bother. Just let us sit wherever we wanted like the cool teachers!

The next order of business was class jobs. This was important. There were four really great jobs: Crossing Safety Officer, Eraser Cleaner, Window Monitor, and Milk Monitor.

The first of the cool jobs was "Crossing Safety Officer." AAA used to sponsor a program at schools where the kids were the crossing guards. Let that sink in for a minute. The kids were in charge of all the crosswalks and directing traffic around the school for the other children. All the guards would get a white reflective belt with a shoulder strap and a badge. It was a real badge! The badges would have ranks on them too! Sergeant, Lieutenant, Captain. They would get a stop sign to hold up to cars and then direct kids to cross the street, AND if a kid got out of line or crossed against the light? You could write them up! With a ticket! How cool was that? The problem was that kind of power would go to kids' heads. One day you'd see a kid as a happy crossing guard, and the next day you'd see them with a black eye because he ratted out a kid for crossing against the light. Once the word got out that you squealed on someone and wrote them a ticket, you would probably get beat up. No one wanted to be a crossing guard anymore.

Another great job to get was Eraser Monitor. Erasers back then were just blocks of black felt. They would fill up with chalk dust and stop erasing, so the Eraser Monitor would have to take all the erasers outside and bang them against the building and knock out all of the chalk dust. That was the only way to clean them. This was a great job because you got to go outside while everyone else was in class! Some of the older kids would spell out dirty words with the erasers on the wall, which was always good for a giggle. When I got bussed to my new school PS 188, I got the eraser job straight away! Nobody even challenged me for the position. I thought, "These kids are stupid! How do you not know how cool this job is?" It turned out that the erasers at PS 188 were foam and not felt like at PS 118, so you didn't have to go outside to bang them on the wall. They had an eraser cleaning machine in a closet. You had to rub the erasers on the machine and it had a loud vacuum that was supposed to suck the chalk dust into the machine. It never worked! The machine was in a closet, so it wasn't vented to remove the dust. The dust would just blow all over this tiny closet. The other problem was the closet was across the hall from the library, and the librarian was mean! She hated for anyone to use the eraser machine because it made so much noise! When you used it, you had to close the door so the noise wouldn't disturb her. I'd be trapped in that closet sucking in all that chalk dust. I was like a nine-year-old coal miner! I guess that was my initiation to PS 188.

Window monitor was another cool job...for someone else! Back then all the windows in our school was about twelve feet high and opened from the top and bottom. Opening the windows from the bottom was easy because all you had to do was push them up. Bingo. Teachers didn't like to do that. We'd throw all sorts of things out those windows! It always started with a paper airplane, but then it progresses to someone's lunch box, books, basically anything that you could get your hands on was going out that window. Teachers rarely opened the bottoms. Opening the top of the window was tricky. The windows had to be unlocked and pulled down to open them. Just above the window frame was a tiny twist lock and in the middle of the window frame was a metal loop. To open or close the window, you had to use the "window pole." A "window pole" was this was a ten-foot wooden pole with a metal hook on the tip. To open the window, you had to hold the pole with both hands, push the window lock to the open position with the little hook on the pole, and then stick the hook in the little hole at the top to pull the window down. So basically they wanted a grade school kid to hold a 10-foot wooden pole with a hook, push a one-inch lock, and then place that hook into to two-inch hole in front of a glass window. See why this job is fun for someone else? Girls would always complain that boys got all the good jobs. We loved for girls to have this job! We couldn't handle that stupid pole, so do you think some nine-year old girl was going be able to control that thing? (Sexist? Yes, but it was damn funny to watch!)

When the weather got hot, the teacher would say, "Window Monitor, please open some windows." Whoever the Window Monitor was would grab the pole and they would look like an acrobat trying to balance that pole! When they would get it over to the window the fun would begin! Since he or she would have to look up the whole time trying to get the hook to unlock the window and then get that hook in the window loop, we'd torment them relentlessly! Spitballs, rubber bands, paper clips, anything we could find to throw them off! And then it would never fail...CRASH! They'd smash the pole right through the window! The whole class would erupt into laughter.

One day when I was in fourth grade, the Window Monitor broke all six windows! Six for six! Then she dropped the pole out the window! Jackpot! I never could understand why teachers wouldn't just open and close those windows themselves? We were scrawny little kids! We couldn't handle that stupid window pole! Secretly I think those teachers knew we couldn't handle that pole and enjoyed the suspense of watching us try to open those windows.

BTW, the record for windows broken in one month? 19.

The coolest of the cool jobs was Milk Monitor. School started at 9 A.M. Around 10:30 A.M we got a milk break. The teacher would sell cookies or pretzels and some kids were on the Free Milk Program. The Free Milk Program was the same as the Free Lunch Program, but only with milk. The thing was someone had to go down to the cafeteria and bring the milk back to the classroom. This was the most coveted job in school! If you told somebody you were the Milk Monitor, they gave you mad respect! When the milk bell rang, you'd get the milk bucket, go down to the cafeteria, grab the milk for the class, and then go back to the classroom. What was the big deal about this job? You were free for as long as it took to get the milk! You could take any route to the cafeteria you wanted! The trick was to get there last, so that way it took longer. Sometimes you'd fool around too much getting there and they'd close the cafeteria! We'd make up some excuse, always blaming it on the teacher. "Mrs. Benjamin couldn't find the milk bucket!" Then we'd wander back to the class passing out milk like conquering heroes! You were greeted like the conquering heroes returning to Rome! "Behold! I returnith to thy classroom and bring forth the silky nectar of the bovine god, that is milk! All hail me!"

In fifth grade I finally got the coveted job as MILK MONITOR! What a day! I had finally arrived! You wanted milk? "Hear Ye! Hear ye! I go forth to fetch thy milk and ye shall be patient and speak my praise in my absence. Upon my return thou shalt shower me with praise!" I forgot to mention, Milk Monitor was a two-man job. They wanted kids to walk the halls with a partner at all times. When you were Milk Monitor you got to pick your partner too! I picked my buddy Robert. Robert was fast like me. We reconnected on Facebook not to long ago and took a long walk down memory lane. He told me all the times we raced he remembers beating me just once. It was the day I wore my brother's track shoes to school and they were two sizes too big. Remember what I told you? Hand-me-downs!

Robert and I were going to change the Milk Monitor game forever. We were going to deliver milk FAST! No more wandering the halls. We were going to run down the stairs, get the milk, and get back in less than five minutes. That was our goal...Our quest...Our mission. The thing was, you weren't supposed to run in the hallways. So we had to be careful not to get caught running. Plus, we had to go right by the principal's office on our way to the cafeteria, so if we dodged that bullet, once we got in the cafeteria we could bully our way to the front of the line. The younger kids would always get to the cafeteria first because they were on the first floor and we were on the third floor. In the history of PS 188, milk had never been delivered so fast! We were in Olympic shape! Then we got greedy.

We were like a great NASCAR team, always looking for a way to shave that last few seconds off our record. What was slowing us down? The milk bucket! Robert and I could fake the run through the halls, and some days we'd get yelled at. We'd slow to a fast walk when in the hallways, but we could flat out fly going up and down the stairs. Teachers said you couldn't run in the halls, but never said anything about running up and down the stairs. Even still…that bucket! Then it dawned on me. The hand railing on the staircase was one continuous railing, and it went all the way to the first floor! What if we connected a hook to the bucket, hook that to the hand railing, and let it slide all the way down from the third floor to the first floor by itself? Would it work? Damn straight it would work! Would it make us faster? Probably not, but how cool would it be to see the bucket going down the stairs by itself! It took a little tweaking, but finally we figured out that if we used a broken wire coat hanger, connected it to the bucket, hooked it on the hand railing, and let it slide, it would stay on all the way to the ground floor! When we let the bucket go, we could stay up with it for about two flights of stairs, but then the bucket would get some momentum and start flying down the stairs! When it would make the turns on the staircase, the bucket would swing way out like a F-16 jet fighter making a sweeping turn! It was the coolest thing I'd ever seen!

It was a Tuesday morning and the milk bell rang. Robert and I took off like a shot! Johnathon was always our timekeeper. We set the bucket on the rail and turned it loose. The problem was, this time the railings had just been stripped of all its paint. They were slick, and they were smooth. The first flight of stairs, we all ran together neck and neck down the stairs. By the time we got down to the second floor, the bucket took off out of our sight. We were flying down the stairs right behind it as fast as we could until we heard, WHAM! "OHHHHH!" As we got to the landing between the second and first floor, we saw the principal lying on the floor holding her head. Apparently what happened was as the bucket swung out coming around the turn between the second and first floor, it came loose from the handrail. It smacked the principal right between the eyes! It was like getting caught at the murder scene with the gun still smoking in our hands. There we were, us running down the stairs, the principal lying on the floor half dazed with the milk bucket next to her head. GUILTY!

Needless to say we were fired as Milk Monitors and banned from ever holding that position again.

Five minutes and eighteen seconds. That was our fastest time ever. We never cracked the five-minute mark. I hope someone, somewhere is telling his kids and grandkids he once delivered milk to his class at PS 188 in under five minutes.

…Without a milk bucket rail slide.

# Every Grade, Something New

Everybody you talk to has one teacher that made a difference in his or her lives. You'll always hear people say, "My third grade teacher, Mrs. Jones turned me around!" or "Mr. Anderson was the greatest teacher I ever had!" Everyone has one of those stories. My son might be the luckiest kid ever. Just about every teacher he had was a gem! He's still in touch with a lot of them (ahh, the magic of Facebook). Everyone has a teacher they admire — except me.

I think I got every "I-Don't-Give-A-Crap" teacher in the New York City school system! In first grade I had Mrs. B. Johnson (there was a Mrs. A Johnson too). She hated me! This was at a time when you could hit kids with a ruler, and she never spared an inch! Mrs. Johnson was flat out mean! Every time she would yell at me, she would close the sentence with "You act this way and your mother is the President of the PTA?"

Second grade I had Mrs. Tenzer. She was *hot*! Not as hot as my brother Vance's fourth grade teacher Miss Shamoney. He tried to kiss her once and my parents had to go to the school! (Nowadays, teachers try to kiss you back!) Mrs. Tenzer played favorites, plus she had my sister years earlier, so all I ever heard from her was, "You aren't as smart as your sister!" or "Your sister always behaved well!"

Side story on the second grade:
One day in Mrs. Tenzer's class a kid named Andrew was acting up. The more she told him to stop the worse he got.

She got up from her desk and left the room. After she came back in the room, Andrew continued to act up. A few minutes later Andrew's mother busted in the door like a one-woman SWAT team. She was dressed in her bathrobe and nasty house slippers. Andrew lived right across the street from the school, so when Mrs. Tenzer left the room, she probably went to the office and called his mother. It only took her a minute to get to the school, and she didn't even take the time to get dressed! She grabbed Andrew and pulled his pants down and gave him the worst whooping I have ever seen! When she finished, she turned to Mrs. Tenzer and said, "Who else is acting up?" She was going to whoop another kid! She didn't care! I guess she figured, "Why come all the way up to the school and just whoop my own kid?" Andrew was a model student after that day. I heard many years later that he was a very successful attorney in the Midwest.

Whooping kids don't work? Hmmmm.

In third grade my brother and I were bussed to another school on the other side of Queens. PS 188. My mother says it was probably the biggest mistake she ever made. I had Mrs. Benjamin. She was about 90 years old and had blue hair! I had never seen anyone with blue hair before! I don't think she had ever seen anyone with an Afro before either! She once accused me of cheating on a spelling test. She made me spell the word, "hospital" out loud to her. It was one of the words on the test. It was the ONLY word I probably got right! She didn't even apologize. I'm glad she didn't catch me!

In fourth grade I had Mrs. Knowles. Mrs. Knowles got sick early in our school year, and we had a substitute everyday.

EVERY SINGLE DAY! Having a substitute teacher was a great thing when you're a kid. You go absolutely crazy! So can you imagine having one for four months? That was my dumbest year ever! I don't know what you're supposed to learn in the fourth grade, but I know we never got around to it! We did absolutely nothing for four months! I blame my lack of progress in my formative years on my fourth grade teacher. I still suffer from that lack of discipline. Good thing Andrew didn't live across the street from that school!

In fifth grade I had Mr. Feinstein. He was nuts! He would smoke a pipe and drink tea in the classroom during class! When we would act up in class he would slam the chair on the floor, his face would turn beet red, and he'd throw us all out the room. These weren't those flimsy aluminum chairs kids have today either. These were heavy wood and steel chairs. He would grab the chair by the side, raise it up, and then slam in to the floor! "GET OUT! GET OUT IN THE HALL!" We'd all run out into the hallway and wait for him to calm down. One day he grabbed the chair and slammed it on his foot. I know it hurt him because you could see it in his face. I guess laughing didn't help the cause that day.

The class across from us was the other fifth grade, Mrs. Zachary's class. They were the class ahead of us. They were supposedly smarter than us. We would have gym class with them and we would whoop their butts in everything. At the end of the year we had a school poetry book made. Mrs. Zachary was the teacher in charge of the book. She used all the stories and poetry from her class, even though I had won a school wide poetry contest with a haiku I wrote. She hated our class. Whenever we got thrown out into the hall, she would look at us in the hall, shake her head, and shut her classroom door like she was better than us. After that, whenever I would pass her classroom I would close her door if it was open, or open it if was closed.

In sixth grade I had Mrs. Pearlman. She was a yeller and a screamer. Anything she would do or say was at the top of her lungs. They used to have a day where the parents would come to class and observe the teachers in action with their students. The day before, Mrs. Pearlman made us rehearse questions she was going to ask us, and she would tell certain kids (yours truly) not to raise their hands while the parents were in the room because she only wanted people who knew the right answers! I put my hand up for every question! She was probably right. I didn't know half the answers, but I thought it was rude to tell us, "Don't raise our hands!"

Seventh grade was the worst teacher of all. Mr. Masher. When I got to seventh grade I was in what they used to call a SPED class. These were kids who scored high on their Statewide Proficiency Exams. We were supposed to be the crème-de-la-crème of the seventh grade. (Before I continue, let me say that I was kind of smart, but you know those kids they always say this phrase to, "You have such potential, if you just applied yourself!" Well, needless to say, I never applied myself!) Anyway, my brother Vance had Mr. Masher the year before me. One day during a math test Vance yelled out, "UGH! Mr. Masher is picking his nose and eating his boogers!" The whole class burst into laughter and disgust. A year later, my first day of class in Mr. Masher's class he says to me, "Are you Vance Jordan's brother?" I said, "Yeah!" He walks over to my desk and leans in towards me and says, "I'm going to make sure you're kicked out of the SPED program!" Wow! Talk about holding a grudge. Did he get me kicked out? Sure did! I'm sure not applying myself didn't help my cause either. Many years later I found out a lot about that guy, and not good things either. Stories for another day's book.

As I wrote this chapter and think back, I probably owe a lot of teachers apologies, especially my seventh grade Spanish teacher Miss Winderbaum. She was *hot* too. She was probably the only teacher I ever had a crush on. I think I was just mad at her because half way through the school year she got married and became Mrs. Walker. That hurt my feelings and broke my heart.

So, to all my grade school teachers, I give you all a heart felt apology.

Except you Mr. Masher.

# The Look and The Call

Before Wal-Mart, before Target, before any of the big superstores there was: Great Eastern Supermarket! Great Eastern was a store in Hempstead, Long Island. It had EVERYTHING! It was the original superstore! It had clothes, food, electronics, a pet store, a bakery, and it even had an arcade for kids! Show me a better store than that anywhere!

Once a week my mother would pile us into the wagon and do her shopping at Great Eastern. We'd get there and she'd give us all a dollar and turn us loose. I don't think she ever worried about us getting lost or someone taking us; people were pretty protective of all kids back then, whether they were yours or not. Besides, who wanted to snatch up four bad black kids? The best thing about going to Great Eastern was we knew that store like the back of our hands! My mother would head off to the grocery department and we would head straight for the arcade. We had a regular routine. First the arcade, then the pet shop, then the toy department, and then a game of hide and seek. Sometimes we would go back outside and have shopping cart races all over the parking lot. After that, we'd go find mom in the grocery department.

All the games in the arcade were ten cents. Skee-ball was my favorite. I once scored a 480 out of a possible 500! Not too shabby! My brothers would play the gun shooting games, and my sister would play this stupid game called "Dancing Bozo." It was a dancing clown puppet. When you hit the buttons, it would pull the strings and make the clown dance and sing the Bozo the clown song. Stupid!

After our money was gone we'd head over to the pet shop and play with the animals, and then we'd head to the toy department and look around.

Great Eastern was BIG! So we'd either play tag or hide and seek. I liked to hide under the dresses of the mannequins. Sounds weird but I never got caught — or maybe they didn't want to admit they knew me! My other hiding place was I used to stand real still next to the mannequins and hold their hands like I was a mannequin. I figured I'd blend in! It must have worked! I never got caught — or, again, they were to embarrassed to admit they knew me!

After that we'd join our mother in the grocery department. She'd have a shopping cart overloaded with stuff! She would say to us, "Stand next to my cart, and make sure nobody takes it." Really? There must have been six to seven hundred dollars worth of groceries in that cart! Who the hell would steal all of that stuff? After a while, my mother would get tired of us nagging her for stuff. "Buy cookies! Get ice cream! Buy me some Brylcreem!" Brylcreem was a hair care product for white people's hair. Back then they didn't have hair care products for black hair. This is before the Afro-sheen and Ultra-sheen craze; mostly we just used Vaseline on our hair. All we had to pick from for hair was Vo5 and Brylcreem. Brylcreem had a catchy TV jingle, "A little dab will do ya!" The guy's hair on the TV would be so lush and wavy. Who wouldn't want to buy some Brylcreem? I'd nag my mother until she gave me…THE LOOK!

Most mothers today don't have this skill. They're too busy negotiating with their children. Who negotiates with their kids? "Stop crying or I'm taking you home! Do you want to go home? Is that what you want? Stop crying or you're not getting a toy! Do you want a toy? Let's get a toy? Okay? You want a toy? Okay first we'll get you a toy, then McDonalds!"

I WISH there was some negotiating with my mom! There was no compromise, no bargaining or haggling — what she says, *goes*! That's it! End of story. If you got out of line you got, THE LOOK! Your mother would give you a stare so cold and so hard that you'd stop whatever it was that you were doing. It was like looking into the eyes of Medusa! You'd turn to stone with just one glance! If you got THE LOOK, she meant business! There was no negotiation, there was no compromise. THE LOOK meant one thing: "You better stop what you're doing because I've had enough!"

Every mother back in the day had her own version of THE LOOK. Some would snap their fingers as they applied it, and some would point a finger as they administered the death stare. There would be times when you'd walk by a kid getting THE LOOK from his mom, you'd turn to look at his mom, and you'd get caught in the gaze too!

THE LOOK is a lost art. Moms just don't have it anymore. I was in New York visiting my parents last month and I said something off color. I'm a grown man and my mother *still* gave me THE LOOK! I was still scared too! Kids know that most threats made today are just that, "threats." They know there will be no repercussions to pay later. No follow through on a vow. If your mother said, "Wait 'til your father gets home!" You could bet your bottom dollar that when your father walked in the door, "Your ass was grass!" If kids act bad today, what do the children say? "What's momma gonna do?" They'll call 9-1-1 and turn you in. Could you imagine calling the police on your parents? You better call an ambulance for yourself too! Your parents may be going to jail, but you'll be going to the hospital. I saw a woman try to give her child, THE LOOK, and the kid gave her THE LOOK right back!

There are a few things I believe in that others don't. I believe there's another earth out there somewhere in the universe just like ours. I can't prove this one, but I believe it. I also believe in time travel, but that I can prove. One day my brother was acting up and my mother gave him THE LOOK. I guess this day my brother figured he was immune to the stare, so he kept acting up. My mother turned to him and said, "If you don't stop, aye swaney I'm going to smack you into the middle of next week!" (I have no idea what "aye swaney" means, but my mother would say it all the time!) Well, I guess my brother was in the testing mood because he just kept on acting up, and my mother spun around and smacked my brother so hard that when the smoke cleared just his shoes were left in place on the floor! He was gone. David Copperfield never performed such a disappearing act! She just continued on shopping like nothing happened. I was speechless! What happened to Vance? A week later we went back to the store, my mother dropped his sneakers on the floor, and he reappeared! He was standing right where she smacked him exactly one week earlier!

Time travel exists. Ask my brother.

I'll tell you something else that doesn't exist today. The call.

I had an Aunt Marie and an Aunt Claudette. Both of them lived in Harlem. My parents would drop us off there to spend the weekends there from time to time. My Aunt Marie would take us to Central Park or Coney Island. My brothers and sister would ride a roller coaster called the Steeple Chase. It wasn't like a regular roller coaster; it was a like a coaster/giant slide hybrid. I never got to ride that ride. My Aunt Marie thought I was too little to ride it. Back then there were no rules on how tall you could be to ride the rides, so I guess my Aunt was ahead of her time.

My Aunt Claudette lived above a bar. My brothers and I would spit out the window and try to hit the people going into the bar. On my Aunt Claudette's block there were kids my age. We'd play football on the sidewalk. Who plays on the sidewalk? I'm from Queens! Football is played in the street! Well, there was no way you're playing football on a busy Manhattan street. Sidewalk football was rough! You had no room to do any moves! Plus, there were people walking up and down the street, so you just played through them and around them. In Harlem, when a parent wanted their kids to come inside for something, they'd yell out the window down to the street for them. That always amazed me. As busy and as noisy as those streets were, every kid heard their parents call them. No matter where they were on that block, they would hear their parents call. It was like an episode of "Wild Kingdom." Penguins as far as the eye can see, but the baby chicks can recognize their mother's call.

Back home in Queens everybody's parent had a different call that we'd hear as well. And the crazy thing was, only you'd hear it! My dad would stand in the driveway and whistle. No matter where I was or what I was doing, if I heard that whistle I would know to head for home. Hopper's mom would stand on the corner and yell, "JUNIOR!" He wouldn't even hesitate — he'd hear that and start running towards his house. Hop got called home a lot because he had a refrigerator with no handle, so it had to be opened with a screwdriver and he was the only one that could open it. He'd get called home every ten minutes! In fact, back then parents would call you in the house for anything! My dad once called me home just to change the channel on the TV! I was so glad when we finally got a TV with a remote control! Another thing I could never understand was my brothers and sister would be IN THE HOUSE, and my father would *still* call me back into the house to go to the store for him! They're standing right there in the house with you! Doing nothing! Why didn't he tell one of them to go? (I'm sure when he reads this book he'll inform me with his logic.)

The best "call home" was for my friend Lance. Lance's father would kneel down at the front door and say, "Laaaannnnccce." It wasn't in a loud voice, just his normal speaking voice. Incredibly, no matter where we were, Lance would hear it! We would be playing a block away, and Lance would say, "I got to go, my father's calling me!" We'd say, "What are you talking about? Nobody's calling you!" Sure enough, we'd look down the block at Lance's house, and his father would be right there in the front door. That's an "Old School" trait that I never could master. When my kids were young I'd call them and get, "Oh, I didn't hear you!" Oh you heard me!

I was in New York a few years ago and we were all sitting outside. My father whistles, and I still turn around.

# Pets

One time at Great Eastern we talked our mother into getting us all hamsters, which I never understood after the "gold fish" incident and she swore we'd never get another pet again.

What's the "Gold fish incident" you ask? We all got gold fish one day for pets. We used to take them out of the tank and play with them on the floor. Some days we'd play "Fish Toss." This was where we'd see how far away from the tank we could toss them back into the tank. One day we took them out of the tank and pretended like we were going to swallow them. I was holding mine by the tail and was bobbing it in and out of my mouth. My brother slapped my hand, the fish slipped from my fingers and got caught in my throat. My mother was screaming and yelling, "What is wrong with you kids! Why would you do something like that? What is wrong with you all!" This didn't help; screaming at a child does not help while he is choking on a goldfish. My father slapped me on my back and I swallowed the fish. My mother wanted to take me to the hospital to have my stomach pumped, but my father just shook his head and said, "No need, it'll come out." (BTW, my brothers convinced me that after eating that fish I could now breath underwater. Yes, you can drown in a bathtub!)

When we got the hamsters, we got the cage, the hamster wheel, the water bottle, and hamster food as well. I think back how smart that store was. It was like a store for people who go to Vegas and say, "I drank all night for free!" but they're five hundred dollars down from gambling! Hand it to them with one hand, and take it from them with the other!

The hamsters were cheap! The cage, the wheel, water bottle and feed were where they got you! After a few weeks of hamsters doing nothing, we invented a game called Hamster Olympics. We'd have them race up and down the hallway, or put them in the bathtub. Yes, hamsters can swim! My favorite event was when we'd put them on the record player. First we'd start at 33 RPMs, then we'd increase the speed to 45 RPMs, and then up to 78 RPMs. There'd be little hamsters flying across the room! One day my brother Gene put super glue on the bottom of his hamster's feet and put him on the record player. He cranked that record player up to 78 and that hamster spun around and around like he was on a runaway carousel! I swear I could hear that hamster screaming for his life! My hamster died after two weeks. I think he committed suicide. Stephanie's hamster died from a poorly constructed parachute accident. Gene's hamster was the victim of a Fourth of July experiment gone wrong. My brother Vance's hamster got lost in the pipes in the house and turned up five weeks later jet black from dirt. You can't bleach a hamster. Those were the last hamsters we ever got.

Years later we got a snake that got lost in the pipes as well. To this day we never found him. Although my parents say they hear him from time to time.

I'm still waiting for that fish to come out.

# Mets Fan – Yankees Fan

I grew up a New York Mets fan. For the most part, people who live in Queens and Long Island are Mets fans. Yankees fans live in the Bronx and Manhattan. (Nobody cares about people on Staten Island!) Most people don't know this, but one of the reasons the Dodgers moved to Los Angeles was because their new stadium was going to be built in Queens. How can the Brooklyn Dodgers play in Queens? Sacrilege! My dad took me to my first ever Mets game.  It was the Mets against the St. Louis Cardinals. Tom Seaver against Rick Wise. We sat in the mezzanine level on the first base side. The Mets lost 3-1. After that I was hooked! I'd go to Mets games all summer long.

The Mets played in Shea Stadium in Flushing, N.Y. "Flushing" was right! Shea Stadium was a dump! Ask any Mets fan and they'll tell you the same thing. It was drabby, had no history, and the planes taking off from nearby La Guardia airport would fly right over the stadium. You couldn't hear a thing! (Years later when I tried out for the Mets, right behind shortstop there was a small pile of dog crap! Are you kidding me? This is a major league field?) The coolest thing about the Mets were they had a song, "The Mets Song."

"Meet the Mets! Greet the Mets! Come on out and see the Mets!" Every true Met's fan knows it. The Mets also had a Mascot, "Mr. Met." It was a guy in a Mets uniform with a giant baseball for a head. Keep your Phillie Panatic or San Diego Chicken! We had Mr. Met!

When a relief pitcher would come in the game from the bullpen, they wouldn't run in from the bullpen to the mound like they do today. They would drive him in a golf cart that had the N.Y. Met's cap as a roof of the cart. How cool was that! And they had a golf cart with the caps of the visiting team too! AWESOME!

The Yankees had a song too, but it wasn't a sing-a-long song like the Mets, and they even had a mascot. The Yankee's mascot was named, "Dandy," as in, "I'm a yankee-doodle dandy." The Yankees' fans hated it so much that they got rid of it after about a week. The east river is very close to Yankee Stadium, so actually I think the Yankees fans made him "disappear," if you get what I'm saying! The Yanks would bring their relief pitchers out from the bullpen in a pinstriped Toyota Corolla. Cheesy!

One day I got Yankees tickets from Mrs. Cramer. The dry cleaners in my neighborhood had a promotion that if you spent a certain amount of money at the cleaners, they'd give you Yankees tickets. It turned out that the people who worked at the cleaners weren't giving the tickets out to the customers! Mrs. Cramer found out and threatened to turn them in, so they gave her the tickets. She didn't have any kids that were baseball fans, so she gave them to my brother and me. They were great tickets too! Right on the rail at third base. Now every true Mets fan knew Shea Stadium was a crappy stadium, an absolute dump, and it always was.

Yankees Stadium (the old stadium) was a shrine! The history, the legacy. Back then they had monuments that looked like grave headstones in center field, ON THE FIELD OF PLAY! How cool was that? Plus, after the game they would let you walk on the field around the edge of the stadium on the outfield warning track and exit the stadium out in centerfield! WOW! It was like walking in heaven! My grandmother lived two blocks from Yankee Stadium, so after the game we just walked to her house.

The Yankees had a third baseman named Jerry Kenny. He stunk! He made two errors in the first inning. The guys next to me were riding him all game. "You stink! You're costing us the game!" It was the first time I'd ever seen a baseball player look like he wanted to cry! Every time he'd go back to play third, they'd get on him. "You hit like my mother! Hey, Kenny! Put a glove on each hand and maybe you'll catch something!" Yankee fans are relentless! This wasn't Steinbrenner's Yankees either. CBS owned the Yankees then and they were worse than the Mets!

Well, I was a Mets fan and all my buddies were too! There was four great days to go to the game: helmet day, batting glove day, hat day, and bat day. And it was a real 28-ounce bat too! A week after bat day, you'd see every kid at little league getting up to bat with their royal blue NY Mets bat. The Yankees had a bat day too. But who wanted to go to the Bronx with 40,000 fans walking the streets with 28-ounce bats? Ever see the movie, *Warriors*? "Warriors! Come out and play!" (Google it.) Years later, the Yankees gave out little wooden Yankee bats that were the size of billy clubs, instead of full size bats. So much better!

My friends and I would go to Mets games a lot. We'd hop on the number seven train to Shea Stadium with our gloves and baseballs. We'd get there early so we'd be first in line to get tickets. We'd play catch or make up some game we called "Way Back." You'd have to throw the ball to someone way up high over his head, and he'd have to turn, run, and catch the ball over his shoulder like you were tracking down a fly ball in centerfield. One day we're out in front of Shea stadium waiting for the box office to open playing "Way Back." The ball goes over my head and gets away from me. As I track it down, I look up and see a baby blue Eldorado Cadillac coming at me with the a front license plate that says, "SAY HEY." It was WILLIE MAYS!

In Mays' later years, he came back to play for the Mets, and he was coming straight at me! Back then the Mets didn't have secure player parking, so the players had to park out in front of the stadium. His car parked right next to me, and he stepped out of the car. There he was, The Great Willie Mays! The "Say Hey" kid! Mr. Basket Catch himself! Sure fire Hall-of-Famer! There was no one around us either — it was just me and Willie Mays! I could barely speak as I walked over to him. "Mr. Mays, would you please sign my baseball?" He took my ball and looked me in the eyes. Then he said in a surly voice, "I don't sign baseballs!" I was stunned! He flipped the ball back to me in the rudest manner. I couldn't move. My idol had spurned me in the coldest way. Now everybody in the parking lot saw Willie Mays and he pushed me out of the way like a rag doll. Mets security had to escort him into the stadium because there was such a mob around him. A few minutes later Yogi Berra came by and signed a ball for me. He couldn't have been nicer! After that day, I hated Willie Mays and the Mets too! When George Steinbrenner bought the Yankees, I jumped ships. He was all about winning and I liked that. Plus, I was a big Reggie Jackson fan and when he came to play for the Yanks that made my day! (Years later I became the biggest Derek Jeter fan!

Greatest Yankee EVER!) I don't hate the Mets the way I used too. I show all my New York teams love — even my stinky Knicks! But I love the Yankees the most.

I've met many sports stars over the years. Some were really nice. George, "The Ice Man" Gervin, Julius "Dr. J" Ervin, Ozzie Smith, both Niekro brothers, Joe and Phil, and I've met some that weren't so nice. Floyd "Money" Mayweather, Rick Foxx, and even Tim Duncan. Yes, Tim Duncan! I'm not a big star (yet), but I always remember the way Willie Mays made me feel that day in front of Shea Stadium. If someone asks me for an autograph or a picture, I never hesitate to give him or her the time. Especially kids. Kids never forget those kinds of things.

Never, Mr. Mays.

# Take A Chance!

I've had three real loves in my life. My High School sweetheart Marshelette, my college sweetheart Jan, and my ex-wife Marilyn. You know where I met them? In person! Marshelette I met in high school when I played on the football team and she was a cheerleader. Classic huh? Jan I met at a dance. She thought I was someone else when we met. And Marilyn I met at a comedy club. She didn't think I was funny!

It amazes me when I hear young couples meet online. People have all sorts of reasons why they choose online dating. They don't like the bar scene, or they're too busy. Busy? I'm a busy man! I work 40 out of 52 weeks on the road. Online dating would be perfect for a person like me. But it ain't! I'll take my rejection in person thank you! I also understand older people meeting online. They don't get to the local watering holes and get-together spots like young people, so online dating might be right for them. But young people? Are kids so lame today that they have to pay hundreds of dollars to sit at home and shuffle through pictures of people they want to send a "Wink" too? Then go on a pre-arranged date by a computer? This is like a play-date without your mommy being there!

One girl told me she liked online dating because she wanted someone who shared her values. Hmmm, you do know they let anyone on those dating sites? AND you can pretend to be anything you want! Catfish! (Google it!) Another guy told me he liked online dating so he could avoid the "crazies." Yeah because there are no crazy people out there on the Internet!

There's a lot of dating sites too. eHarmony and Match.com are the two biggest, and then there are specific dating sites like J-Date.com for Jewish people, and ChristianMingle.com for Christians. I love their commercials, "Find God's match for you!" I don't think God is worried about making matches on the Internet! Especially not for a fee.

There are free sites like Plenty-of-Fish.com and Cupid.com, and then there are sites for older people Our-time and Seniors-meet.com.
There's also one for really old people called, "who-the-hell-is-left.com." That's the one my son suggested for me. (I ain't laughing!) Have they removed the romance out of romance? I went on a date where the woman was on her phone the whole time! I kept thinking maybe she's checking her Match.com page to see if there was a better choice out there. I may get rejected a lot...A LOT! But isn't that the price you pay? You roll the dice and take your chances! Every old time romantic movie goes like this: boy meets girl, boy loses girl, boy gets girl! That's just the law of nature! Not, boy texts girl! Girl swipes left!

Is this the conversation we're going to hear from now on?
     "Hey, how did you two meet?"
     "Well, I was lonely and too afraid to go outside, so I paid $79.95 to get on a website. I was rifling through pictures of women for months and I came across her picture. She said she was fun and enjoyed life — I could tell that just from reading her profile on the website. As it turns out, I'm fun and enjoy life too! What a coincidence! What are the chances of two people saying they are fun and enjoy life? I sent her a 'Wink,' which is a way of

telling her I was interested in her, and she sent me a 'Wink' back. Then I sent her a 'Gift,' which was a vase of flowers sent to her profile that cost me another $9.99, and she sent back a smiley face emoji. Then I texted her for about a month, and she texted me back. We finally met for dinner, talked for a bit, and then I texted her goodbye."

It was love at first profile. Don't laugh! That day is coming! Roll the dice kids, step up to the plate and take your swings! If you see someone you like, take a chance! Say, "Hi!" Start a conversation. Tell a joke, ask him or her to dance, you just might be amazed what happens! Babe Ruth struck out 1330 times. Do you think anyone remembers that, or even cares? Nope! He's remembered for how many home runs he hit. (714 just in case you didn't know)

So what's the moral of the story? Get off the internet and get in the real world. Meet people, have a conversation with someone you don't know, and join the rest of civilization. It's not that bad!

There's going to come a day when I go to a wedding, the bride and groom stand in front of the minister and when asked, "Do you take this person?" they'll text each other, "I DO."

Don't laugh. That day is coming.

# Everybody's Music Stinks!

One of the things my generation complains about the most is the music of this generation. I'm sure this is a trend that is older than mankind. I'm sure when Moses was wandering the desert there were kids singing whatever the song of the day was and Moses was probably complaining, "What the heck are they singing? Is that even music? What's wrong with these kids?" You know what? This needs to stop. Music is music, is music, is music. I grew up in the Disco era, big horn bands, and The Jackson 5. I loved (and still do) Earth, Wind and Fire, Chicago, Tower of Power, and great bands with big horn lines. (If you ever see me around ask me about the time I opened for Tower of Power.)

I loved Disco too! Disco was HOT. You play a Disco song and watch me hit the dance floor! The Latin Hustle, The New York Hustle and the Bump. That's dancing! There were some really big Disco stars back in the day too, as Donna Summers, Chic, Gloria Gaynor, and I loved it! We had big afros, giant collared shirts, big bell-bottom pants, and we walked around with five-inch platform shoes. These were the men! Before all you kids start laughing, any fashion looks better than what they have today. Pants sagging off your butt like you have a loaded diaper. Nobody wants to see your draws. Pull your pants up!

There was a football player on the Pittsburgh Steelers named Frenchy Fuqua and he used to have platform shoes with a live goldfish in the heel! (You've got to Google it!) One Easter my brother bought a purple and lavender jump suit with purple platform shoes. SUPER FLY! Saturday night fever was a huge movie that came out of the Disco era. In that movie they do a dance called "The Bus Stop." Really? You know what that dance is called today? "The Electric Slide!" It ain't nothing new! AND I defy anyone to name me a bigger movie based on a music era than Disco. The movie, "Beat Street Boogaloo?" No! "Breaking" 1 or 2? Hardly! Disco ruled!

Some say the band, "The Knack" killed disco with their song, "My Sharona." Others say Disco died July 12$^{th}$, 1979 at a Chicago White Sox versus Detroit Tigers double-header. Fans were allowed into the stadium for 98 cents and a disco record. The plan was to blow up all the records between games and end disco forever. Well, 90,000 fans showed up to the game, and half of them ended up on the field! That didn't workout the way they planned! BTW, some say Rock died in the 90's. Where are all the great rock bands? AC/DC? Zeppelin? Guns and Roses? Metallica? I asked my daughter-in-law who her favorite rock band was, and she said, "Maroon 5!" I threw up.

I think the thing that bothers me the most about music today is, there are no instruments and they can't sing. A lot of the music is synthesized or "sampled." (Google it.) Plus artist who can't sing get their voices "cleaned up" in the studio. They don't even sing their songs in concert; they LIP SYNCH! In concert! I saw Rihanna in concert and she only sang about half her songs! It was more of a dance show than a singing concert. To flip the coin over "P!nk" was on the bill too, and she was amazing! When old school songs come on the radio I always tell my kids, "Wait! You hear that? It's real instruments in that song with real singing!" Now, I could go on and on telling you how great my generation's music was with examples of the greatest band for every genre:

Greatest boy band ever? Jackson Five! And they played instruments!

Funk music? How about Parliament. Or the funkiest man on the planet: PRINCE! He's not my generation, but he's damn funky!)

Rock? Hendrix. Steppenwolf. The Who.

R&B? Aretha. Stevie Wonder. James Brown. I feel good!
I could go on and on about why MY generation had the best music EVER! By far!

That being said, I can't say that the music today is all bad. There does seem to be more crappy music out there than ever before, but that may be due to the fact that there's just more music and avenues for artists than there was before. Bigger pool, more crap. Simple math.

There was a study done that said the Hip Hop music of today has been more influential on society than the Beatles and the whole European invasion of rock was in the 1960's. I don't know if I'm smart enough to qualify that study. A lot of Hip Hop and Rap does seem to reflect the times we live in, but didn't a lot of the music of the 60's and 70's reflect the time? "Sex, Drugs and Rock and Roll" was the battle cry of the day. We had songs about the war, songs about poverty, and even songs about everything that's still going on today. I'll tell you what, I don't know a lot, but I know this, when I'm humming a tune or hear someone singing in an elevator, it's usually a 60's or 70's classic. It's rare when I hear someone humming "Big Booty Girls," and I can assure you, Frank Sinatra's "My Way," is requested at karaoke way more times than "Thong Song!"

I had a music teacher in junior high school named Mr. Hamburg. He was one of the few teachers I really liked. He was honest, fair, and sarcastic. What more could you ask for? He hated Elton John. He used to ask me, "Why does a guy so talented waste his time playing *Now* music? He always called top 40 music "Now music." He would say, music on the radio is only relevant "now;" none of it will stand the test of time. In three months you won't even remember it. To his point, there's a Billy Joel song called "The Entertainer." It a song about a singer and what he has to go through to be successful in his business. In that song he has a couple of lines, *"Today I am your champion, I may have won your hearts, but I know the game, you'll forget my name, I won't be here in another year, if I don't stay on the charts,"* or the line, *"If I go cold, I won't get sold, I'll get put in the back in the discount rack like another can of beans.*
That sums it up.

"You listen and hear Elton John. You teach and learn Beethoven"
- Mr. Hamburg

My son has over six-thousand songs on his iPod. Six-thousand! All of it is contained in a in a little gizmo that he can carry around in his pocket. Wow, who ever thought that's where we were heading? When I was a kid everybody had a giant stereo in their living room. Some even had a TV in the center of the console that would be huge! If it didn't work you would just put a smaller TV on top of the broken one.

At that time we played records...in stereo! That was a big thing, Stereo! Two speakers. Music out of each channel and that was high tech! You could put on a stack of records and listen to music all night. 33's, 45's. (78's were before my time, but my dad still has a closet full of them.) Every 45 had a "B" side. One side of the record had the song that was the "hit" song, and the "B" side was usually a crappy song. We bought 33's, or albums, the most. Albums had about fourteen songs on them, usually seven on each side. Albums were great because the covers were works of art! Some of the most famous bands are known by their album covers. Beatles? Abbey Road. Need I say more?

The really good bands would put out a double album. Two records! They would fold open with a record inside each half. Plus, a double album was perfect for cleaning your nickel bag of marijuana (so I've heard). When you first got an album you couldn't touch it. You could only handle it on the edges. This would last about a week, or until someone bumped the record player and scratched the record. That was the fatal flaw in records: they'd scratch, break, warp, skip, and get static. Sometimes the needle on the record player would get dull, and as everybody knows, you tape a nickel on the record arm to give it more weight. But how could music get any better?

Then came the 8-track stereo. 8-tracks were square cubes about the size of a thick sandwich with an audiotape inside. You would push it into a slot on the 8-track player and pick one of the four tracks to play. A whole album on an 8-track cassette? How can it get any better? They even put 8-track players in cars! The problem was, you couldn't rewind a song that was playing. You could only fast forward. Plus, it wouldn't wait for a song to be over before a track would switch. Sometimes it would change tracks in the middle of a song. 8-tracks were big and thick, but they were still portable. That was high tech!

After the 8-track craze came cassettes tapes. Tapes were a lot smaller than the 8-track and easier to carry. Cassettes were great because not only were they small, but you could also record music! WHAT? Record any song I want? How many guys made a mix tape for a girl? Raise your hand! Cassettes were around for a long time. Why not? They were high tech! They even launched a music player craze. First there was the cassette player, which was a little portable player that would play your music. Then came the boom box. This was a huge portable stereo player, and I mean huge! And it was LOUD! You'd see guys walking the streets with this massive boom box on their shoulder blasting music in their head. You could hear it three blocks away. No wonder hearing aids are such a big business now.

People became smart and moved away from the boom box to the Walkman, which was a personal compact cassette player that you could wear on your belt. It also allowed you to plug in ear buds so that only you could hear it, instead of the entire east coast. Could this be the zenith of music? What could be any better? Cassettes had its downfalls as well. The tapes would break or twist inside the cassette. The worst part was if the cassette player was dirty, it would "eat" the tape and you'd have to try to pull the tape out of your player without breaking it. Everybody knew the second best thing a pencil was used for was reeling in the tape back into the cassette.

There were also some very short-lived attempts in music technology. There was the 4-track, but I don't think anyone bought that. Quadrophonic stereo was a record player with four speakers that you would put in each corner of the room and it would play each instrument through a separate speaker. I though it was great. My brother-in-law had one. The problem was it would only work with Quadrophonic records; otherwise it was just a regular stereo system.

So, cassette tapes? Does it get better? Time marches on! Out came the CD, or compact disc. This now had to be the holy grail of music reproduction! They were thinner than records and more durable than tapes. You know how many songs you can get on a CD? Lots! And you can play every song without having to flip it over! Finally, Nirvana! The CD was going to be the end to all ends. They even made them recordable, so what could go wrong? This was surely the best music could get, right?

When CD's were first introduced the promise was since they would cost half the price of a cassette tape to make, they'd be half the cost. I think that lasted a month. Record companies actually charged more for CD's. Their reasoning was that since people were already accustomed to paying more for CD's, why lower the price? Plus, they weren't as indestructible as were lead to believe. They'd skip, scratch, and break just like records. But we all threw away all our cassettes, Walkmans, and followed the new leader: CD's.

That was until the microchip. This was the game changer. The microchip allowed music to go digital. Music was now clean, no flaws, no skipping, no annoying tape, and you can play your music on almost anything! Your phone, MPG player, stereo system, AND you don't have to be near the player. You can play it wireless! HALLELUJAH! We have arrived! Well, the problem with digital music is it's closed every record store in the world. All music is bought online now. Artist put out albums, but who buys albums anymore? There used to be a day when a group put out an album and there would be about eight to ten songs that were really good. An album could stay on the charts for months because they would release a song from the album every few weeks. Now people buy *a* song. *One.* For $1.29 at that. It's rare if an album even has more than one good song today! Now here's the real kicker, music people say now that "Vinyl," or "Records" is the best way to listen to music because of its flaws. Records are now the rage! We've come full circle! I hope you didn't throw them away!

My father used to yell at me about my music. (Still does) "How do you listen to that? Its just noise! Bling, blang, blong!" My dad is a big Jazz fan. Dizzy Gillespie, Art Blakey, Miles Davis. He'd play his records all day on Sundays. Some of it I liked, and some of it sounded like bling, blang, blong!

When I listen to music today, some I like, and some? Well...

I like all music. Country, Rap, R&B, Rock — there's good and bad in all genres of music. When I was a kid my brother-in-law Gerald had a band called, "The Fifth

Estate." They would rehearse at my house in the basement. When they would go play gigs, my parents would take all of us to the dance where they were playing. I would sneak on stage and play his Congo drums. (Gerald would always correct my pronunciation, "It's pronounced, '*Coon-ga* Drums!'") He knew I was on stage with him, and I know I sounded horrible! But he never said anything. Guess that was my introduction to the stage.

I bet all parents have a problem with their kids' generation of music. Rock and Roll was going to be the death of civilization! Rap is killing our youth! I'm sure in Beethoven's day, his father sat at his piano and said, "What is that noise you're playing?" It sounds like bling, blang, blong!" Ad infinitum!

Another problem I have with today's music is the vulgarity. I'm no prude. Some of it I even like. But can you disguise it a little better? Remember Marvin Gaye's song "Sexual Healing?" Here's the lyrics:

*"Ooh baby, I'm hot just like an oven*
*I need some lovin'*
*And baby, I can't hold it much longer*
*It's getting stronger and stronger!*
*And when I get that feeling*
*I want sexual healing*
*Sexual healing, oh baby*
*Makes me feel so fine"*

That's pretty racy! But here's the difference, I can sing that all day in public and not offend a soul! We all know what he's saying! It's *how* he's saying it!

Here's a song by an artist named, "Big Sean." The name of the song is, "I Don't F**k with You."

*I don't f**k with you*
*You little stupid ass bitch, I ain't f**kin' with you*
*You little, you little dumb ass bitch, I ain't f**kin' with you*
*I got a million trillion things I'd rather f**kin' do*
*Than to be f**kin' with you.*

Believe it or not, this was a number one song on the radio! Of course they edited out the dirty words for radio play, which is pretty much the whole song! Can you imagine singing this song at Karaoke? Or anywhere else in public? Number one song. It boggles the mind.

Dirty lyrics in a song don't offend me, and if that's what you like, that's fine. Like I said, it's just music. However, if it's music that may offend someone else with its lyrics, then you should play it so only you can hear it. I don't need to be in my car at a red light and hear your radio blasting three blocks away about a girl with a big ol' booty!

There's an old saying, "If it's too loud, you're too old." I guess I'm officially, "too old."

BTW. I have one son that likes Country, another that likes Rock, and another that likes everything. I think I did something right.

In the end, it's all just, bling, blang, blong.

# My Turn!

When I play games with children I never let them win. NEVER! I don't care how old they are, and I don't care what game it is — I Never Let Them Win. I know that sounds mean, but here's my reasoning. There's going to come a day, and I promise you it'll be sooner than you think, that you cannot beat them at anything!

I used to play Scrabble with my son Kevin. I would try to keep the game close, but when I'd see the tiles running out, I'd start putting together longer words worth more points and pull away at the end. Another victory for me! That lasted until he was about ten years old. I would even try to cheat with the score, but he caught on to that pretty quick. After that it took all I had to beat him, and when I did, it was because I got lucky!

I'd play golf with my son Johnny. When he was younger, I'd give him lots of strokes so that he'd have a chance to win. Now he's giving me strokes! Lots of strokes! And I need them too!

My nephew James is always asking me for a rematch for a race we had when he was young. I gave him a ten-yard head start and beat him by ten yards. Every time I see him I make it a point to bring up that race. I don't dare give him another shot at me. He'd give me a ten-yard head start and beat me by twenty!

At my grandchildren's house they have game night. One night we were playing a game called "Trouble." (Remember that game?) You have to roll the dice, actually the die is in a bubble called the "Pop-O-Matic." When you press down on it, it would make the die jump, and then you move your pieces around the board until you get them all back to the base. "Trouble" has rules, as do all games, but here are the "House Rules" they've added:

- You can move any piece at any time, which isn't in the rule book.
- If you land on another person, they don't have to go back to the start, which *is* in the rulebook. (It makes the children upset when they have to go back to start, so they took that rule out.)
- If you get a number you don't like, you can roll again. WHAT?
- And, here's the craziest house rule of all, EVERYONE gets a chance to win!

Needless to say, that last rule wasn't going over well with me! Everyone gets a chance to win? Why is this generation so hell bent on everyone winning, everyone gets a trophy, everyone feels good and gets a hug? I won every game of "Trouble" that night. I am proud of it and make no apologies about it! I even talked smack!

When we were young, we'd play board games all the time. My sister was the absolute master at the game "Clue." "Colonel Mustard in the library with the pipe!" She'd never miss! We used to play Monopoly a lot too. Everybody has "House Rules" for Monopoly. One of the rules we added was all the money you had to pay to the bank, went under free parking, so whoever landed there got to collect all the money. My ex-wife's family played if you got the "Advance to Go" card you got paid twice. That was stupid! Unless you got the card! I always lost at Monopoly, mainly because I would trade my good properties for the railroads. Railroads in Monopoly are worthless! My sister would get me to trade Boardwalk and Park Place for B&O and Reading Railroad. What an idiot! I should have at least held out for the Electric Company!

One of my favorite games to play as a kid was "Sorry!" Sorry was a lot like "Trouble" except the board was bigger and there was no dice. Cards would tell you how many moves to make. Sometimes you could land on a spot where you could *slide* your piece to the next spot. If there was someone else's piece on the *slide,* you could send them back to start. The best part was when you sent someone back to start, you didn't just bump them off the board, you'd say, "Soooorrryyyy!" and slam their piece across the room! That's the way we played. Somebody won and somebody lost. Just like real life. Everybody didn't get a chance to win. If you won, you knew you earned it and deserved it. No second chances. If you didn't like your move, there were no special rules. Crying? Are you crying? There's no crying in "Sorry!" There's nothing wrong with losing. You learn more from losing than you do from winning. Plus, losing makes winning that much sweeter! Ask Chicago Cubs fans if they ever win!

Why are we still giving kids trophies for just participating? NFL Pittsburgh Steelers linebacker James Harrison recently had his six and eight-year-old children return their trophies because they were trophies for just "participating" and not actually winning anything. I can't stop applauding him enough. This is another thing that has to stop, and the "no one's keeping score" nonsense. Believe me, EVERYONE is keeping score — even the kids! At my parent's house, all of our trophies are in the living room. (Especially that stupid MVP trophy my brother won in high school.) Every single one of those trophies are for winning something. First, second or third. Everyone else? Try harder, see you next year. They don't give out participation ribbons at the Olympics! Why do we teach our kids that mediocrity is as good as superiority?

When we played games on 113th road growing up, sometimes we won, sometimes we lost. That's life. There's a famous scene in the movie "Meet the Fockers." Robert DiNero says to Dustin Hoffman (talking about Ben Stiller's childhood trophies):
"I didn't know they make 9$^{th}$ place ribbons?"
"Oh Jack, they got 'em all the way up to tenth place!"
Problem is, they have them all the way up to 20$^{th}$ place. Sucks to come in 21$^{st}$ place I guess.

You ever play video games with kids? Watch their fingers. They're like lightning! And they can play all day — they have thumbs of steel! The Xbox 360 has about sixteen different buttons you can push to cause an action on the screen. Sixteen! You know what the Atari system had? One! One button, one joystick. That's it. If you wanted to jump? One button. Run faster? One joystick. Simple. You play today's systems and you feel like Dustin Hoffman in "Rainman" trying to keep up with all the buttons you have to push. I play Call of Duty with one grandson and Lego Superheroes with the other. I get crushed by both of them. By the time I figure out what's going on, on the screen and what button to push, I'm toast. Up, down, right stick, power up, A, A, over, double click… "Yeah, one minute to Wapner. I'm an excellent driver, excellent driver."

I used to be pretty good at video games. Especially the greatest video system ever made: The Atari 2600 game console! That was single handily the greatest gaming system of all time, and I had them all! Pong started it all! I had the Atari 2600 and 5200 systems, the Intellivison system, Sega, Sega Saturn, Sega Genesis (horrible system), Game cube, and 3DO Interactive (which was a system ahead of it's time). I had Nintendo. Remember how you fixed the games? You blew into them! I also had Super Nintendo, Nintendo 64, Dreamcast, ColecoVision, Playstation 1, 2, 3 & 4. Xbox, Xbox 360, and Xbox One, which is really the third Xbox, but it's called "One," and a Wii. Wii was going to revolutionize the gaming industry because instead of sitting all day playing, you had to interact with the characters on the screen. You move, they move. Great idea until the people started throwing their controllers through the TV screens. If I had half the money back that I spent on all those systems...

Well I could say that about everything I collected including baseball cards, comic books, and Matchbox cars. You know you're officially old when you start every sentence with either, "Remember when," or "Way back when, if I had just..." Maybe I should get my mom really, really mad and she can give me the "LOOK" and then smack me so hard that she knocks me back to the middle of the last century! "Aye Swaney!"

Every video game my grandkids play are "shoot-em up" games. Call of Duty, Battlefield, Grand Theft Auto. Remember the games we played? Frogger? Your job was to get a frog across the street without getting squished. Donkey Kong? Climb up a maze of ladders to rescue a girl who is being held by a giant gorilla who is trying to stop you by throwing barrels down on you. (You don't think they were smoking something funny when they invented that game do you?)

My grandkids don't like playing board games or some video games with me because I don't let them win. Why should I? Their day is coming. My daughter-in-law always says to me, "Do you feel good beating a seven-year-old?" Yes, I do!

I figure I got about three more good years.

# Curfews

Do kids even have curfews anymore? I don't think so. Usually mom drops them off at the mall, movies, or wherever they hangout nowadays, and then they call their mom when they're ready to go home. It's like having your own personal limo service. My kids had bedtimes. At least the first two did. After the youngest one was born, we were too tired and worn out by the first two fighting over bedtimes. We didn't even bother fighting with the last one about his bedtime. We'd let him stay up as long as he wanted to until he fell asleep. You know what? He was a straight 'A' student, and never missed a day of school. Who knew? Maybe the secret to good grades is just let them stay up and watch the Tonight Show!

I don't remember a time when I didn't have a curfew. When we were young, the streetlight was the timer for everyone in the neighborhood. When the streetlight came on, that was the signal for everyone in the neighborhood to go in the house. One day we figured if the streetlight didn't come on, we could use that as an excuse to stay outside longer! So we spent the entire day throwing rocks at the light trying to break it. Do you know how hard it is to throw a rock straight up in the air and break a streetlight? AND not get hit by the rock coming back down to Earth? I'm sure if we had broke that streetlight the next day, Mrs. Richardson would have had the news stations all over Queens! "You know I saw dem Jerden boyz throwing rocks at the streetlight. I know it was that little one who broke it!"

In the summertime or weekends, we got an extended time to be out. When the light came on we had to be in front of our house. This was a vague instruction because "in front of the house" could mean next door at the Celeste's house, down the street at the Branches' house, or across the street at Bobby's house. Sometimes we'd be in someone's house, and we'd call home and make a lot of noise in the background so they'd think we'd were having so much fun that we couldn't come home. That never worked.

As we got older, we were given a specific time to come home. And I do mean *specific*! "Be home at 11!" That meant you better had been home at 11! Not 11:30, not 11:15, and not "I was in the driveway at 11." Whatever time you were told, that's the time you had to be *in* the house. Sometimes you'd try to reason with them, "Frank and Hopper don't have to be home until 11:30!" This was always countered with, "Then go live at Frank and Hopper's house!"

At my house, when you came in the house, you had to come in the side door, make an immediate left, go up a small flight of steps, make a right handed u-turn right at my parents' bedroom door, go through the dining room, then head upstairs to our rooms. The problem was the side door was noisy when you opened it, and the first flight of stairs in front my parent's bedroom squeaked. So if you were a little late, they'd hear you trying to sneak upstairs. Why didn't we use the front door? We didn't think about that until years later when we had girlfriends. The side door was never locked, so getting in the house wasn't a problem. As you tried to sneak up the stairs and make the turn at my parents' bedroom door, you'd always hear them call your name, "Kevin is that you?" Dang! Busted!

"Yea,"

"What time I tell you to be in this house?"

"Eleven."

"You know what time it is?

"Eleven-Thirty."

"Don't be coming in this house all hours of the night like you grown! Your mother was worried sick!"

It was always funny to me that my father did all the yelling, but it was my mother that was always worried sick!

One time I snuck into the house and heard this:

"Vance?" my father yelled.

Holy crap! They didn't know who was sneaking in the house!

"Yea?" I responded.

"You know what time it is?"

"Eleven-Thirty."

"I told you to be in at eleven!"

Holy smokes! It was working! They thought I was Vance! Then they threw me a curve.

"Is Kevin with you?"

What could I say? Apparently nothing. I froze!

"Kevin is that you?" he asked.

Dang! Double busted! Needless to say, I got in trouble, and I got Vance in trouble too. I should have learned to throw my voice!

One of the worst times I got caught coming in late was when I went to a basement party. I loved basement parties! Regular parties were usually upstairs in a living room or dining room, and the parents would pop in and out to check on things. Sometimes they'd even have grandma or one of the little kids on patrol during the party. Basement parties were in the basement, they'd turn the lights down real low, and play slow dance music. Usually at a basement party, girls would let you dance real close. Well, as close as you could get before biology took over and things were "rising to the occasion." Then every guy was dancing with his butt stuck way out so he wouldn't be embarrassed.

My brother Gene caught me practicing once with the pole in our basement. Hey, a guy has to prepare! To this day I wear my belt buckle to one side because I thought when I danced with a girl she would mistake the buckle for a different part of my anatomy. Yes, I was an idiot! Basement parties were also hot and sweaty. Nobody in New York had air conditioning in their basements. Imagine the smell of 40-50 sweaty kids in a hot basement? That had to be worse than the New York Jets' locker room!

The big thing at those parties was to bring gum so your breath wouldn't stink, but we smelled like wet dogs anyway from all the sweat! Our breath was the last thing we should have been worrying about! At the end of the party, you tried to get one of two things: a girls phone number or a kiss. For me a kiss was out of the question — I was too shy! Hell it took me six weeks to kiss the girl I eventually married! Getting a phone number meant you had to be tricky. You didn't want to ask one girl for her number, and then get caught by another girl that you just got a number from! Half the time you didn't even call the girls you got numbers from — you just wanted to get her number! That was the trophy!

This one particular night I had a chance for a kiss! A KISS! Frank and Hopper were pushing me to get it too.

"Man, what you waiting for?"

"Yea Kev! You see she waiting for you!"

"Man if it was me? I'd be over there right now!" Well I went over there with legs like jelly and nothing to say. Twenty minutes of standing there I got neither the kiss I wanted, nor the phone number I deserved. The whole walk home that's all we talked about.

"Man you should have kissed her!"

"I know! Her friends wouldn't leave us alone!" I replied.

"Yo, you should have told her friends, 'Excuse me, we have something to finish.' That's what I would have done!"

How come friends never do anything things themselves, but always tell you what you should have done?

I remember that night I came home five minutes late. FIVE. I reached for the side door to open it, and it was locked. This threw me because the side door was never locked, and no one had a key either. I knew the front door was locked, and I couldn't climb in any windows, so what could I do? I did the one thing no kid wants to do when they're late getting home — I had to knock on the door. No kid wants to do that! Have your parent let you in and confront them at the door? No way! I tried and tried to get that door to magically open, but a locked door will not open. (Now I know!) So I broke down and knocked. Very lightly. I figured if I knocked lightly my mother would wake up and not my father. That's kids logic. That didn't work, so I knocked again harder this time. I could hear my parent's bedroom door open and I could hear someone coming down the stairs to open the door.

"Who's that?"

Crap! It was my father! Oh well, I'll just suck it up and take my medicine.

"It's me, Kevin"

"What time is it?"

I remember standing outside thinking, "Were we gonna play this game? Can't you just let me in?" Okay, let's get this over with.

"It's five after eleven"

"What time I tell you to be in this house?"

"Eleven." I would have made it too, if I hadn't waited so long to try and kiss that girl at the party. I should have told him that! Then I heard my father walk back up the stairs and close his bedroom door. I knocked again, no answer. I knocked even harder, still no answer. He wasn't going to let me in! Over five minutes late? What was I going to do? I went around the corner to Hopper's house. I figured I'd sleep there for the night. I rang Hopper's doorbell and his mother answered the door. "WHO'S AT MY DOOR!"

Mrs. Hopper only had one tone of speaking, LOUD! She was nice, but she scared the heck out of me! I once saw her throw a can of Carnation Milk at Hop and hit him square in the butt! POW!

"It's Kevin, Mrs. Hopper can I…."

"Kelvin?" She always called me Kelvin. "What time your daddy tell you to be in the house?"

"Eleven Mrs. Hopper, but…"

"What time you get home?"

"Five after Mrs. Hopper."

"Well I can't help you. Your daddy tell you to get home at eleven and you boys think y'all can come home anytime y'all want, then stay out there on the street!"

Holy crap! She wouldn't let me in HER house because I was late getting home to MY house! My father had the whole neighborhood in on it too! Every friend's house I went to nobody would let me in! I went back home and got the key to the station wagon. My dad had a key hidden in the wheel well of the car and I slept there for the night. The next morning my dad got in the car to go to work. He didn't realize I was in the car until he was about four miles down the road. Or did he?

Years later my son Kenny went to a party. I told him to be in by twelve o'clock. At twelve-fifteen he comes home and I had double locked the door so he couldn't get in. He rings the bell and knocks on the door. I talked to him through the door.

"You know what time it is?"
"Twelve-fifteen."
"What time did I tell you to be in this house?"
"Twelve."

I thought about it for a minute and opened the door. As he walked by me he says, "Sorry." Then he says, "You look just like grandpa standing there!"

He's lucky I only "look" like grandpa.

# Let's Get Ready to Rumble!

I don't always agree with the things that I see today, compared to the way they were. Maybe I'm just getting old(er), or as my son says to me every time we have a discussion on, "what was" and "what is," he'll say, "Yeah, yeah. I know, 'get off my lawn!'" I'm not THAT old! Yet!

My daughter-in-law has a unique method for handling her three boys when they start fighting. When they're fighting, or after a fight she tells them, "Hug your brother! Hug him!" I tell you what, I can see in their faces they don't always want to do it, but it sure calms them down. Granted they're two, six and seven years old. Let's see how that works in ten years!

As silly as I think that is, I sure wish my parents had instilled the "hug" policy at my house when I was a kid! My brothers and I wouldn't fight, we would *FIGHT*! Brawl, donnybrook, scuffle, clash, melee, rumpus, scrap, battle and wrangle! Call it what you want, it was every man for himself and survival of the fittest. Ever see a wild-west bar fight? We called that Tuesday afternoon at the Jordan household! We didn't care if there was company over our house, or if we were out in public — if something set you off, the bell rang, your dukes went up, and you would commence to fighting!

I was the youngest, so I was going to take the brunt of the punishment. The youngest always does. When my father would hear us fighting, he would just yell at us. "You want to fight? Go outside in the backyard and fight! I'll put a boxing ring out there and you can kill each other!" I didn't need a boxing ring. I needed a corner man to throw in the towel to keep me from sustaining any more punishment! One of the things my brothers liked to do was drag me to the banister over the staircase and threaten to drop me down a flight of stairs. Gene would usually have compassion and pull me back up, AFTER I said "uncle" a hundred times or swore that I'd 'never do whatever it was I did. (That would last about a week.)

Vance on the other hand wasn't as strong as Gene. He'd hang me over the banister and make me yell "uncle" and beg for forgiveness, but his arms would get tired and instead of pulling me up to safety, he'd just let me go. If you've never fallen down a flight of stairs let me tell you, you don't just pop back up like in the movies. It hurts! Back then, when I went to school with black eyes and bruises all over my body, nobody said to me, "Are you being abused at home?" They'd just say, "Which brother did that to you?" Some days we would fight and I'd go crying to my mother. Let's face it, moms are way more compassionate than dads. Mom would put a stop to this madness and keep me from getting beat to a pulp, right? Nope! I'd go crying to my mother looking for some sympathy and retribution. Here's what I'd get:
        "Vance, get in here!"
Vance would come in the room looking sad, like something happened to him!
        "Yes?"
        "Did you do this to your brother?"
        "He hit me first!" A classic response in any household.
        "I don't care who hit who first! Don't do that to your brother. Understand?"
        "Yes." Then Vance would leave the room.

That's it? No spanking? No weeks of punishment? I'm holding my eye in my hand and all he gets is, "Don't do that to your brother?" To make matters worse, she'd turn to me and say, "Leave your brother alone!" WHAT? Leave your brother alone? Do you see my eye here in my hand? Do I look like the winner of this fight? I'm the victim here lady! The worst part is, I've violated the code of the house. I went crying to mom, and I snitched out my brother. You think the beating I just got was bad? I had to go back upstairs and deal with whatever new retribution that was coming my way. Usually it was the silent treatment, or the "I'm not touching you" torture. Don't know what that is? Someone says, "Don't touch me!" Then the other one would proceed to put their hands as close to the face and body of the other one and say over and over, "I'm not touching you!" I once heard a swarm of horse flies buzzing around the head of livestock will drive it mad. Imagine a pair of dirty hands just millimeters from your face for hours on end and the constant rant of, "I'm not touching you!" That will drive you mad. And the fight starts again!

My father, in his infinite wisdom, found some boxing gloves and brought them home. Really? You'd bring boxing gloves home and put them on the table where you knew we would see them? Deep down I think my father liked it when we fought! Every now and then, and because I wanted "Real Justice" instead of "Mom Justice," I would go crying to my father. His response always was, "So? Hit him back!" Oh, I'm sorry, have we just met? My name is Kevin, I'm your youngest child. I'm going go back to my room, hit him back, and then get dropped down a flight of stairs. Please call the ambulance now! My father had to know what would happen when those boxing gloves came in the house!

My brother's wanted to have a boxing tournament. Here's how it would work. First me and Vance would fight. The winner would move to the championship round, and then the loser (me) would have to fight Gene. I tried to get out of this by saying I would just be the referee for their fight, but this was to no avail. I was on the fight card. If you've ever felt a boxing glove, they're rather soft. This won't be so bad! It'll be kind of like a pillow fight where the pillows are on your hands. Right? WRONG! I've been punched in the face with and without boxing gloves. I'll take no gloves everyday! A glove is big! And the bigger the glove, the more space it covers on your face! Most kids don't know how to throw a punch with a fist, but with a glove you don't have to. When that glove lands, it blankets half your head. Ever been knocked out cold twice in one day? I have!

One day I had had enough of getting beat like a rag doll. I went to my father and told him as much. His reply? "Hit him back!" I would plea, "I've tried to him them back — they just beat me up more!" Then my father gave me the one piece of advice no father should never tell his son to do to his own brother. He told me, "Hit him in the man zone, and he'll leave you alone." That is absolutely forbidden in a family fight. Heck, in a real fight it's an unwritten rule that you don't hit a man below the belt. But I had been given the green light to go low, so ring the bell, pardon the pun, and I couldn't wait!

I remember the day like this. I was at the side door and Gene was at the top of the stairs and wouldn't let me pass.

He was really just joking around. It wasn't really a fight, nor was it punch worthy, but I was given the green light to punch out the family jewels and I was going to use it! Gene kept blocking me as I tried to get past him. Then he made the fatal mistake. He stood there with his hands on his hips, legs spread, smugly looking down on me. "What you gonna do now?"

Ever see a Popeye cartoon where Popeye eats the spinach and then his fist grows ten times it normal size? That's what it felt like when I reared back and unleashed the uppercut punch so picture perfect that Mike Tyson would have been proud. I saw my brother double over in excruciating agony and fall to his knees. I knew better than to stand there and admire my work, so I tore out of the house and ran down the street. I must have run ten blocks before I realized Gene wasn't chasing me. Had I done it? Had I exorcised my demons? Ten minutes later I walked back into the house and Gene was still doubled over in pain. My father walked in behind me and said to Gene, "What's wrong with you?"

All Gene could eek out was, "Kevin hit me in the balls!" My father looked at me and said, "Don't hit your brother in the balls." Then he went on up the stairs. All my life I had heard my brothers get the, "Don't hit your brothers" line. Now I got it, and it felt good!

Gene beat me up many times after that and dropped me over the banister many more times, but it didn't matter. For that one day, that one instant, that one moment in the Jordan household, I got to hear,
"Don't hit your brother."

My "get even" day with Vance wasn't as sweet as my "get even" day with Gene. If I had hit Vance in the "Man Zone" he'd still be beating on me to this day! Like I said, Vance has a short fuse. He wouldn't do something destructive or criminal, but if he's doing a task and you're not onboard with the way he's doing it, or not up to the task of doing it *his way*, you're going to feel his wrath!

This one morning we were cleaning our room. Vance would push the broom and I would hold the dustpan. We were just about done. Actually, in my eyes we WERE done, but again, this is my brother Vance we're talking about. We couldn't get that last line of dirt into the dustpan. You know that little line of dirt that won't go in the dustpan no matter how hard you push the broom? That line of dirt! Vance kept yelling at me that I wasn't holding the dustpan at the proper angle to get the dirt in the pan. I said, "You just don't know how to use the broom!" With that, Vance popped my foot with the broom. This was not your ordinary push broom either. It was a big heavy wooden broom. All the tools and appliances my father would buy were big and heavy! Brooms, shovels, picks, rakes — these were tools for plowing the back forty acres! I burst into tears and my father came upstairs.
   "What the hell is going on up here?"
Through my tears I blubbered out, Vance hit me in the foot with the broom!" I think it was one of those days where my father was fed up too. He told Vance, "Put your foot out, and let him hit you back!" Vance stuck his foot out and I looked at my father standing there. I remember thinking, "Is he really going to let me do this?"
Then my father gave me the go ahead. "Hit him back!"

I grabbed the broom and swung it over my head like I was driving in the last spike of the east meets west railroad! Just as I was about to make contact with my brother's foot, he pulled it back about two inches, just enough to make me miss his foot. Good thing too! I hit the floor so hard with that broom, I put a dent in the floor that is still there today. I would have shattered his foot if I had connected. I knew it, Vance knew it, and even my father knew it. There was an awkward silence seconds after the explosion of the broom hitting the floor. I could see Vance's whole body trembling, my father looked at him, and then looked at me. "Fine! Now you're even! Knock off this stupid noise up here!" He looked relieved that I missed his foot as he walked back down the stairs. Vance did too! I was mad I missed, but I'm glad I did.

My dad should have come upstairs and said, "HUG YOUR BROTHER!"

I wish.

# Now What?

"The children now love luxury. They have bad manners, contempt for authority; they show disrespect for elders and love chatter in place of exercise."
– Socrates, 399 B.C. (Before Cell Phones!)

Are the kids today smarter than we were? Maybe, if you judge intelligence by how well you can navigate your life around a computer. By that measure they're all Einstein's!

I played golf once with a guy who told me he was a grade school teacher for forty years. I asked him, "What's the difference between the kids today, and the kids when you started?" Two holes later he gave me an answer. He said, "You know, the kids are about the same. Kids are kids. I think the biggest difference is the parents." He went on to tell me that when he first started teaching, if he had a problem with a child, he'd call home, and that night he knew that problem was dealt with. Today, you either can't get a hold of a parent, they're blaming the teacher for picking on their kids, or the kid is calling his parent on their own cell phone! And the truly sad part is, I said "parent," and not "parents." The single parent household accounts for one-quarter of all households in the U.S.

Remember when we went to school? To get an 'A' on a test you had to get a 100%? Now it's 80%! How is 80% an 'A?' That's a low 'B' at best! When my nephews were in middle school they had to take a class called, "Self-Esteem" class. Really? This is a class? Exactly how do you teach, "Self-Esteem?" Show them SNL sketches of

Stuart Smalley? (That's actually a funny joke if you…Google it!)

My nephew told me that the teacher would come in the class and tell them a sad story. Then she'd start crying. Two years later I asked his younger brother about the class, and he told me, "All that woman does is cry everyday!" Now this woman either has the saddest life of any human alive, or she's the greatest actress on the face of the earth! Either way, what a freaking scam! But someone on some school board deemed this class necessary.

What happened to the three "R's?" Reading (W)riting and (A)rithmetic. Okay, we wanted it to sound good phonetically, not be correct literally. I remember a teacher once saying to me, "If you can read, write, and add, everything else in life will fall into place." How true is that? If you wanted an 'A' you had to work harder for it! Reach up and get the bar! You felt better about yourself for getting it! Don'y bring the bar down where it doesn't mean as much because you don't want to hurt their feelings. There are some schools that can't use red ink on a paper because red ink symbolizes something bad. There are schools that let kids write essay papers where spelling doesn't count! Can you believe that? SPELLING! They get graded on content, not grammar. I wrote a paper in science class once and got a 'C.' You know why? Too many misspelled words! When I argued my case to the teacher he told me, "Every teacher is a English teacher first."

Now you may think this is just at the grade school level, but my mother was a professor at Adelphi University. I was watching her grade papers. Just to mess with her I asked her, "Do you grade on a curve?" (Believe me, without the curve I'd still be in college!) She says, "I will now!" What happened was, she said that a student came to her office and said that if she didn't get an 'A' that she would lose her scholarship. The problem was that that paper was horrible! Bad grammar, poorly structured, and this was a graduate student! I said, "Are you going to give her an 'A?' She told me, "If I do, I have to change everyone's grade." Where was she when I needed an 'A?'

We keep making things easier for kids. Play sports? Don't keep score, and everybody gets a trophy. Homework? No homework on Fridays because we don't want to stress them out. Exercise? Just an hour — we don't want to overburden them. Heaven forbid they sweat. Should we put all the blame on the kids? Of course not, someone created this environment. Sometimes the mirror tells all, parents!

Would I want to go back and be a twelve-year-old kid again? Maybe, only if I can ride my bike without a dorky helmet. Or if I break up with my girlfriend, I'd like her to tell me face to face, not have to find out by checking her status on Facebook.

Speaking of Facebook, I like Facebook! I get to see what my friends across the country are up to, I've reconnected with people I haven't seen for years. My son likes to say, "His generation likes Facebook to stay connected with their friends, my generation uses Facebook to re-connect with friends." That's partly true. I like some of the groups on Facebook as well. There's some just for comics, some for actors, and I even found one about my old neighborhood, Jamaica, Queens! Amazing some of the pictures that turn up, or even some of the information that gets shared. Let me say this also, just because you read it on Facebook, does not make it the truth!

My niece loves to "hashtag" everything she writes on Facebook. "I went to the beach today and had a extra cheesy burrito! #Beach, #Today, #Cheesyburrito!" First off let me say this to all the kids all over the world:

1. Nobody cares what you ate today so quit taking pictures of it! #Stopit
2. You're tired today? So what! We don't need to know every little aspect of your life! (First get a life and THEN we'll be interested!) #Nobodycares!
3. If you disagree with someone's opinion on Facebook, remember, "IT'S JUST AN OPINION!" Like the old saying goes, "Opinions are like butt-holes, we all have them and they all stink!" #Getalife!

Here's something I would love to see on Facebook, "You know, after reading what you wrote on your wall, I realize how totally wrong I've been all these years and totally agree with you!"

4. QUIT HASHTAGGING EVERYTHING!

Nothing you say is that important that I have to follow it for days on end! (In my day, if I said someone was following me, there'd actually be someone behind me! Trust me on this one, not everything you're saying, writing, or think about needs to be regurgitated over and over for your own self-indulgence! #Enoughwiththehashtags!

You know what's even worse? You ever talk to someone who uses the word "hashtag" in his or her verbal conversation? "I went to the mall and couldn't find a single thing to wear! hashtag searching, hashtag back-to-the-mall!"

"Mr. Jordan, you're charged with punching the defendant in the mouth for no reason and you're pleading not guilty?"

"Yes, your honor. The defendant was talking to me, and at the end of every sentence he would say hashtag-this, or hashtag-that! Then he took a selfie, and posted a picture of his lunch on Facebook, and kept nagging me to "Like" his page, so I punched him in the mouth."

"I see your point Mr. Jordan. You're free to go! Hashtag innocent!"

Please, I beg of you. Stop with the hashtags! #Nomorehashtags, #Noonecares

A few weeks ago I was at a dollar store. I saw one of those old balsa wood airplanes I used to build as a kid. You would fly it by winding the propeller, which is powered by a rubber band. I took it to the park, and as soon I let it fly, kids gathered around me to watch. This simple plane flying around amazed them. They were all asking for a turn to fly my plane. I went back to the store and bought twenty more. (They were a dollar!) I gave them to all the kids in the park. The parents all gathered around and we all reminisced about flying those planes as kids. We talked for hours about all the games we played, the toys we used to play with as kids, some of the crazy things we did to our parents, and the price we paid for it! But you know what we all agreed? All the trials and tribulations we went through as kids made us better adults and stronger people. We climbed trees, played ball day and night, we went out and made friends on our own, we created jobs in our neighborhoods, and made up games to play.

We watched Saturday morning cartoons, and had to come in the house for dinnertime, and then we'd sit around the TV as a family and watch "Combat," "Ed Sullivan," even the "Flintstones!" People forget the Flintstones was originally a prime-time evening show, much like the Simpsons! And we didn't go blind from sitting to close to the TV either!

It's funny when you go back home to where you grew up. You recognize everything, but nothing looks the same. Same houses, same street, but it's almost unrecognizable. I always walk out of my parent's house and expect to hear one of my friends calling me to play football or see my sister and her friends jumping double-dutch in the street. Where are the kids going by riding a Stingray bike with the banana seat and sissy bar? Or kids standing in a circle playing, "one potato, two potato," to see who was going to be "it" in a game of hide and seek?

My parents still live in the same house I grew up in. They've been there close to sixty years on 113th road. I've tried to get them to move to Florida like every other New Yorker, but they refuse to go. "Why would I move? I know where my doctor is." That's my dad. My mom still does consultant work. Eighty plus years old and still gets on the bus and train and goes to Brooklyn to work. "Retire and do what? Sit around and get old?" That's my mom. They're both true New Yorkers. Born and raised in Harlem, and moved to Queens when my brother was born. How New York are they? If you watch any show on TV that's about New York, they will tell you what street in New York they're on, who used to live near there, and what restaurants are nearby. That is the honest to God truth! Watch an episode of Law and Order with them and see if I'm lying!

Side story:
My father wanted to go back to Harlem and video where he lived and went to school as a kid. My father, my son Kevin, and I walked the streets of Harlem as he narrated for us. He pointed the block he lived on and where his school used to be. We came across an old Jazz club. As we walked up to the club, a walking tour of Harlem came by. There was a guy with about twenty-five people following him as he talked about the sights and streets of Harlem. As they got to the club, my father took over the tour. He told them all about who used to play there and what would go on in the club. He even did a little Q&A. Even the tour guide was impressed with my father's presentation. As they were leaving a few of them had looks on their faces like, "Why isn't this guy giving us the tour?"

I think that the truly sad part is thirty years from now, some parents will get together in a park somewhere and watch their kids stare at their phones, and all they'll reminisce about the days they sat around a TV and played video games. Then they'll get in their flying cars and fly away.

I sure Hope I'm wrong. About the first part — flying cars would be great.

But you know what? You're probably too young to understand, so what do I know? I know this;

When the street lights come on, it's time for everybody to go in the house.